# Under the Radar

*of related interest*

**Women and Girls on the Autistic Spectrum, Second Edition**
Understanding Life Experiences from Early Childhood to Old Age
*Sarah Hendrickx*
*Foreword by Judith Gould*
ISBN 978 1 80501 069 2
eISBN 978 1 80501 070 8

**My Autism Journal**
*Carly Jones, MBE*
ISBN 978 1 83997 434 2

**Safeguarding Autistic Girls**
Strategies for Professionals
*Carly Jones, MBE*
*Foreword by Dr Luke Beardon*
ISBN 978 1 78775 759 2
eISBN 978 1 78775 760 8

**Supporting Spectacular Girls**
A Practical Guide to Developing Autistic Girls' Wellbeing and Self-Esteem
*Helen Clarke*
ISBN 978 1 78775 548 2
eISBN 978 1 78775 549 9

**Taking Off the Mask**
Practical Exercises to Help Understand and Minimise
the Effects of Autistic Camouflaging
*Dr Hannah Louise Belcher*
*Foreword by Will Mandy, PhD, DClinPsy*
ISBN 978 1 78775 589 5
eISBN 978 1 78775 590 1

# Under the Radar

## An Essential Guide to Autism and Girls

### Dr Emilia Misheva

Foreword by Dr Carly Danesh-Jones, MBE

**Jessica Kingsley Publishers**
London and Philadelphia

First published in Great Britain in 2024 by Jessica Kingsley Publishers
An imprint of John Murray Press

3

A CIP catalogue record for this title is available from the
British Library and the Library of Congress

ISBN 978 1 83997 448 9
eISBN 978 1 83997 449 6

Printed and bound by CPI Group (UK) Ltd, Croydon, CR0 4YY

Jessica Kingsley Publishers' policy is to use papers that are natural,
renewable and recyclable products and made from wood grown in
sustainable forests. The logging and manufacturing processes are expected
to conform to the environmental regulations of the country of origin.

Jessica Kingsley Publishers
Carmelite House
50 Victoria Embankment
London EC4Y 0DZ

www.jkp.com

John Murray Press
Part of Hodder & Stoughton Ltd
An Hachette Company

# Contents

*Foreword by Dr Carly Danesh-Jones* . . . . . . . . . . .    7

*Preface* . . . . . . . . . . . . . . . . . . . . . .    9

1. Flying Under the Radar: Autism,
   Girls and Diagnosis . . . . . . . . . . . . . . . . .   13

2. School and Education . . . . . . . . . . . . . . . .   45

3. Friendships and Relationships . . . . . . . . . . .   67

4. Puberty, Menstruation and Personal Care . . . . . . .   85

5. Mental Health . . . . . . . . . . . . . . . . . . .   97

*Conclusion* . . . . . . . . . . . . . . . . . . . . 125

*Endnotes* . . . . . . . . . . . . . . . . . . . . . 129

*Recommended Reading and Resources* . . . . . . . . . . 137

# Foreword

I am thrilled to introduce Dr Emilia Misheva's crucial work, which provides a robust overview of the experiences of autistic girls and women, backed up by academic research.

As someone who has worked alongside the autistic community since 2008, and as an autistic woman myself, I am intimately familiar with the challenges our demographic faces, as well as the lack of evidence-based research available to support our calls for change. Too often have I offered insights from either my personal perspective or from years of advocacy work only to be asked in response: 'Where's the reference? Where's the research?' This question, while understandably stemming from a desire to ground recommendations in data, has also helped contribute to the erasure of autistic women's realities. The absence of citations has enabled some professionals to conveniently overlook reported struggles rather than partnering with autistic advocates to further investigation.

Dr Misheva's work answers the vital call to explore the experiences not just of autistic people generally, but of autistic girls and women specifically – a group who have for too long been left out of the conversation around what it means to be autistic. This text moves beyond the standard criteria we often associate with a clinical autism pathway to bring light to crucial yet overlooked areas like hyper-empathy, camouflaging behaviours, perspectives of gendered differences in autistic expressions and the impacts of puberty and adolescence on those assigned female at birth.

By thoroughly citing research on autism while centring the real-life complexities of what it means to be autistic and female in this world, Dr Misheva makes visible years of collective advocacy. This work has the power to shape diagnostic processes, improve mental health support systems, and transform educational accommodations for generations of young autistic girls so that they no longer need to spend time justifying their own lived experience. I cannot overstate what a game-changer this overview is, both for validating lived expertise and providing a launch pad for future meaningful impact, driven by the actual concerns of the community. Bravo, Dr Misheva, and thank you.

*Dr Carly Danesh-Jones, MBE*

# Preface

## The 'double-empathy' problem – or why I wrote this book

When two people who experience the world very differently meet, they are *both* likely to have some difficulties with understanding and empathizing with each other's perspectives, at least to begin with – this relatively simple idea is also known as the 'double-empathy' problem[1,2] and it raises particularly important questions when we consider how autistic and non-autistic people communicate with each other. Research has indicated that non-autistic people struggle to identify the emotions of autistic people and judge them negatively when meeting them for the first time[3] yet this is rarely spoken about or portrayed as a 'deficit' on non-autistic people's part.

And yet, autistic people's differences in this very area are often presented as a key, defining 'deficit' that needs to be addressed through intervention, so that they can successfully 'integrate' in society. Questions about what *neurotypical* people may need to do to adapt to a diverse society where not everyone shares their neurotype are rarely, if ever, raised. More often than not, the onus is on autistic people and their families to advocate for themselves, to adapt to structures developed by and for neurotypical people and to fit the very restrictive mould of what is considered 'typical' or 'normal' by neurotypical standards.

In that context, understanding the needs of a group of autistic people that has often been rendered invisible and whose needs are still routinely missed or misunderstood is critically important. Autistic girls and women have historically been marginalized on several levels – their needs were, up until recently, almost absent from the academic literature, as autism was wrongly perceived as a 'male' condition, and while there is growing recognition of autism in girls and women now, there is still a very long way to go.

The purpose of this book is twofold – I hope that it will be helpful for autistic people, people who think they might be autistic, their family members, friends and professionals. However, it is also intended for those who know very little about autism and who may think that they don't know any autistic people – the onus to educate ourselves is on us all. The simplistic 'them' and 'us' narrative is unlikely to change while the literature on autism is perceived as being for a 'specialist' audience. Trying to understand the different ways people are or can be is meant to be a two-way street and a collective responsibility.

*Chapter 1* will consider the ways in which the needs and profiles of autistic boys and girls sometimes differ, with a focus on the role of different gender-specific societal norms, expectations and stereotypes. We will consider whether it is appropriate, and, indeed, accurate, to refer to 'male' and 'female' autism and will explore the characteristics of the 'internalized presentation of autism' as a more useful way of making sense of some autistic girls' needs.

We will also explore why, for a long time, the experiences of autistic girls and women were excluded from the dominant narrative and their needs were, and to a great extent still are, poorly understood. Finally, we will focus on the diagnostic discrepancies between autistic boys and girls and will address questions such as why girls are less likely to be diagnosed with autism, and why they score lower on the 'gold standard' diagnostic assessments.

*Chapter 2* will consider autistic girls' needs in education, including how those may change and evolve from primary to secondary school. We will explore how a lack of language and learning disabilities or difficulties could further mask autistic girls' needs in school and result in incorrect assumptions about the source of their differences.

*Chapter 3* will focus on friendships and relationships, and how the internalized presentation of autism in girls may influence the way autistic girls approach social interaction. We will discuss one of the most common misconceptions surrounding autism – the myth that autistic people are unempathetic.

*Chapter 4* considers the various changes that take place during puberty and the unique challenges this tumultuous period can pose for autistic girls and young women.

*Chapter 5* explores autistic girls' mental health needs and considers how delayed diagnosis or lack of recognition could lead to misdiagnosis or 'diagnostic overshadowing'.

Finally, a word of caution: it is important to remember that no two autistic people are the same and, much in the same way as we shouldn't assume what a person's individual needs may be based on their diagnosis alone, we shouldn't make assumptions purely based on their gender either. Therefore, while the book focuses on presentations that we may come across more often in girls, the ideas and conclusions drawn are likely to be relevant and applicable to all children who fit the same profile, regardless of gender.

# CHAPTER 1

# Flying Under the Radar

## Autism, Girls and Diagnosis

Autism is so much more than just a few stereotypes that are presented to us. When people think of autism, they think of young little boys who are obsessed with trains. And although that is the reality for some autistic people, we are a lot more diverse than that single representation. The world we live in needs to understand that there is not one way to be autistic, and that you cannot automatically tell who is autistic based on their gender or appearance.

*SB, autistic woman*

- It has been estimated that *80% of autistic girls are still undiagnosed at 18.*[4]

- Autistic women are *13 times more likely to die by suicide* than non-autistic women.[5]

What is the first thing that comes to your mind when you think of autism? For many, it is a boy who struggles with friendships but loves trains and is very good at maths. For others, it may be a male TV character such as Sheldon from *The Big Bang Theory* – a highly intelligent theoretical physicist with limited social skills and a penchant for professing his intellectual superiority, who is very literal in his understanding of the world. While not solely responsible for it, popular culture has long perpetuated the reductionist trope of the 'autistic genius' – typically male, usually socially awkward, often direct and abrupt, with little understanding or regard for social conventions. These traits tend to be portrayed with an undertone of judgement, either as personality 'quirks' at best or as character-defining flaws at worst, which may be perceived as peculiar by others, but are ultimately 'redeemed' by the character's prodigious intellect.

Not only does this stereotype fail to reflect the much more diverse and nuanced reality of the many different ways of being autistic, but it also perpetuates several problematic misconceptions. First, it largely or completely ignores the fact that autistic people, just like any other people, can be highly sensitive, kind, caring and empathetic; those qualities, however, can be expressed differently by some autistic people. For example, some autistic children may attempt to comfort an upset family member by bringing them a favourite toy, snack or drink, rather than by hugging or physically comforting them, if they find close physical contact uncomfortable. Second, it implies that autistic 'traits' are negative by default and can only be elevated to a tolerable 'quirk' if the autistic person also possesses qualities, skills or talents that make them socially useful, such as high intelligence levels, meticulous attention to detail and the ability to solve problems that seemingly no one else can. Third, it fails to reflect the full range of diversity within the autistic community, and the fact that, while some autistic people are indeed highly academic, others have accompanying learning difficulties or disabilities; similarly, while some autistic people are very verbally articulate, others have language and communication differences and may use alternative modes of communication. Finally, it perpetuates the simplistic and misleading stereotype of autism as a 'male' condition that manifests as an extreme version of supposedly 'typically male' traits and interests, which renders invisible the diverse experiences of many autistic people who do not fit this very restrictive mould, regardless of gender.

Understanding how autism is portrayed in the media and in popular culture is important. While it may be tempting to dismiss these stereotypes as being of little relevance to autistic people's day-to-day lives and the process of obtaining a diagnosis, they tell us something about how autism is perceived in society and what has come to be accepted as 'the norm'. We are all influenced by the societal and cultural messages we are exposed to, to varying degrees. This also applies to the adults who are in a position to refer children and young people for specialist assessments and support – their parents, carers, school staff and other childcare and education professionals. For them to be able to identify that a child may need an autism assessment, they would first need to have a general awareness of the different ways of being autistic. If they have come to believe that autistic people are predominantly male, abrupt, prefer their own company and spend their time playing with trains, would they be able to recognize autism in girls or, indeed, in any child who does not conform to this stereotype? Even highly trained professionals are far from immune to these messages, especially if those are also replicated in the academic literature. They can also directly affect the experiences of autistic young people and their parents, who may need to challenge misconceptions about themselves or their children stemming from these stereotypes, such as acquaintances enquiring if a non-speaking autistic child with moderate learning difficulties is 'secretly a maths genius' or disbelieving a girl's diagnosis on the basis that she 'doesn't look autistic' because she can maintain eye contact, has friends and is verbally articulate.

## Is there really such a thing as 'male' and 'female' autism?

In recent years, we have learnt from both research and the accounts of autistic people themselves that the experiences of autistic boys and girls can, in fact, be very different.[6,7,8] Some autistic girls, particularly those with no accompanying language and learning difficulties, have more subtle and less immediately obvious needs compared to boys. This does not necessarily mean that there is 'male' and 'female' autism, though – that would be too big an oversimplification. An (imperfect) analogy to illustrate this is height – while women are, on average, shorter than men, it wouldn't really make sense to talk about 'male' and 'female' height – that would be far too simplistic. Rather, it is more useful to think about those differences from the perspective of *externalizing* and *internalizing* autism presentations, where the latter is more common in autistic girls and women.

Specifically, some autistic people may '*externalize*' their distress in a way that is visible to those around them, whereas others are more likely to '*internalize*' their distress or 'keep it all in', often at a great cost to their mental health. For others, a combination of the two may occur in different contexts – 'keeping it together' at school or at work, and releasing all the accumulated anxiety and distress in the safer environment of the home, which could then be labelled as 'anger issues', 'aggressive outbursts' or mental health issues or even 'parenting issues', none of which would fully and accurately capture the underlying causes and may lead to inappropriate support. It is important to emphasize that many autistic people, regardless of gender, internalize and mask their difficulties; however, this presentation does seem to be more common amongst girls and women, based on what we know from research.[9,10,11] This, in turn, could mean that autistic girls' needs and differences in many aspects of their lives remain unrecognized or misunderstood (see Figure 1.1).

Autistic girls who fit the more 'traditional' – if there was ever such a thing – externalizing presentation of autism may have needs that are easier to spot; they may also need a high level of support on a daily basis from a very early age, which would make their differences easier to detect – and diagnose. While many autistic girls without language and learning needs need support too, their needs are often more subtle, making them less easy to spot, until they have reached a crisis point – and often when they are in the later stages of primary school or in secondary school. The case studies that follow Figure 1.1 illustrate this.

## Communication, interaction and friendships

- May smile, make 'appropriate' eye contact and have a good understanding of social norms and expectations
- Being verbally articulate may mask full extent of difficulties
- May have one or two close and intense friendships: any issues with those may result in considerable distress
- May copy or attempt to memorize different social rituals, phrases or behaviours in order to fit in – may use films, books, interviews, social media for reference

## Education and learning

- May seem to be 'doing okay' in school but returns home exhausted and burnt out, which may lead to school distress
- Difficulties may be seen as only affecting home initially, particularly in the early stages of primary school
- Anxiety may become more pronounced in secondary school or later stages of primary, when the demands, complexity and intensity of social interactions with peers increase
- Special interests may not be detected as such if they fit gender stereotypes (e.g., books, fashion, movies, intense fascinations with particular musicians or actors)

## Emotional wellbeing

- Undiagnosed autism may be mistaken for mental health difficulties
- Anxiety may be (wrongly) perceived as a 'female trait' and thus trivialized by adults: the full extent of the anxiety and its impact on day-to-day life may go undetected
- May be wrongly diagnosed with conditions such as personality disorders and bipolar disorder – signs of being overwhelmed may be perceived as 'emotional instability'. This is known as 'diagnostic overshadowing'
- May find school overwhelming and even traumatizing, and be unable to attend
- Situational mutism

## Sensory processing

- May present with a less overt sensory-seeking profile – i.e., quietly overwhelmed by sensory input but no external manifestations of distress
- May avoid activities that are overwhelming or unpleasant on a sensory level (e.g., brushing or washing hair, brushing teeth)
- May have difficulties identifying internal bodily sensations, such as thirst or hunger, or be very aware of others (feeling of having food in stomach)

*Figure 1.1: Internalized presentation of autism*

## AMIRA

Amira is a five-year-old girl who recently started school. She is not using language to communicate; however, she uses vocalizations, pointing and taking adults' hands to convey her needs. Amira prefers to play by herself and school staff say that she likes to engage in activities 'on her own terms'. Amira is very sensitive to noise and likes to explore her environment by touching objects and surfaces; she finds immense joy and pleasure in water play and pressing her skin against cold surfaces. Amira's needs were spotted as soon as she started nursery, and she was referred for an assessment shortly after. She was diagnosed with autism at the age of four. School staff are very fond of Amira and say that she is a lovely girl who seems happy and content most of the time, as long as her needs are being met by attuned adults around her.

## ELLA

Ella is 13 years old and attends a mainstream secondary school. Ella's primary school had no specific concerns about her and described her as a quiet and shy girl who was doing well academically and would always work very hard. Ella's primary school reports praised her for being very studious and conscientious, and highlighted her love of reading as a key strength. Ella would often be spotted on her own in the classroom during break times, usually reading a book, much to the delight of adults, who would comment on how 'good' and 'mature' she was.

Ella would often worry a lot about tests, changes in routine, her teacher not being in, disappointing school staff or whether her friends liked her – but she kept those feelings to herself. However, as soon as she got back home, she felt exhausted and wanted to be left alone because she was so tired from bottling up all her feelings and worries during the day. This became harder and harder for Ella to hide in the final two years of primary school and Ella would tell her parents that she had a tummy ache in the morning and asked if she could stay at home.

When Ella started secondary school, she found the new, bigger and much noisier school, frequent teacher and classroom changes and complex friendship dynamics completely overwhelming. Attending school became exceptionally difficult for Ella and, after pushing herself to go to school regardless, she became burnt out and was no longer able to leave the house. This was initially seen as a discrete mental health problem and she was diagnosed with anxiety. While Ella was, indeed, highly anxious, this did not go to the root cause of her problem and the therapy she was offered was not suitably adapted to the needs of neurodivergent people. Further attempts to make Ella attend school proved very traumatizing for her, her difficulties intensified and she became depressed and suicidal. At this point, a new member of the mental health team working with her queried whether she might be autistic. She was referred for an assessment but, due to the 18-month-long waiting list, her family sought a private assessment and she was subsequently diagnosed with autism.

As we can see from these case studies, to recognize the internalized presentation of autism in a timely manner, we need to be able to consider the young person's experiences from *their* perspective, rather than just the impact their differences may have on those around them. It is also important to consider how our preconceived ideas of what is 'normal' or typical behaviour in girls – e.g., 'girls worry more than boys'; 'boys are boisterous, girls are quieter', etc. – can stop us from seeing clear signs that an autistic young woman may have social communication differences or be in quiet distress. Similarly, it is also important to consider how those difficulties may be seen as 'not an educational problem' if the young person is academically able and, as such, they may remain undetected until a crisis point is reached.

---

Being high-masking does not mean a person is better off. We have spent a lifetime trying (often in vain) to hide our differences so that no one else will see all the things which are hard for us. You may mistake an inability to self-advocate as politeness, people-pleasing as affability, and our nerve-wracked perfectionism as easy high achievement. You may incorrectly assume that high marks in school or having a job means we will have similar successes in other arenas: that we can intuit how to navigate relationships, to manoeuvre out of awkward or dangerous situations, or to manage the many demands and unpredictable events of adulthood. As solitary problem-solvers, we may shut down or go somewhere else in our minds during high-stress situations. We rarely show a trace of our internal struggles and visceral emotions pent up inside of us, like internalized shame, chronic doubt, worry, indecision, confusion and feelings of alienation. Our brains are constantly on overdrive in social interactions, analysing whether we are getting it right, trying to gauge whether we've made any social gaffes, and if so, what – often coming up answerless. You could say I have been both privileged and not at all privileged to be able to meltdown in private. I suffer deep emotions and rumination, most of the time. Because I can mask, and often don't know how to process and express my emotions in real time, others have had no glimpses into my inner world. It's difficult to convince people that I am disabled, that my capabilities are highly variable day to day, and that I am in need of help.

*KD, autistic woman*

This does, however, also raise broader questions about autistic girls and women who haven't reached a crisis point, or who are coping reasonably well, and are thus unlikely to be diagnosed. While seeking a formal diagnosis may or may not be what they want or need to pursue, recognition of autism should not be dependent solely on whether the young person is struggling so much that they are showing visible signs of distress or not coping. Recognizing that you're autistic can be very helpful, even if you haven't reached a crisis point, as it offers the opportunity to understand yourself better (which may help prevent a crisis point being reached in the future). However, a diagnosis, in and of itself, doesn't guarantee that the child's needs will be met, unless the adults and professional services around them commit to giving them the support they need.

## Autistic girls and diagnosis

A lifetime of feeling different. Years of traits neatly packaged under (best case) anxiety or (worst case) alien. And then, what should have been matter of fact but felt like a miracle: I was assigned a doctor with experience of how autism presents beyond genders. A doctor who wasn't ticking off a list of deficits or bound by myths and stereotypes. Within minutes of meeting, she saw me so clearly. Not for how I was broken, but for who I am: magical, sensitive, autistic.

*Jolene Stockman, autistic*

---

Autistic girls and women tend to get diagnosed later in life, score lower than boys on autism assessments and have to show a broader range of difficulties to receive a diagnosis.[12] Girls are also more likely to 'camouflage' their autistic traits by using masking behaviours to compensate for their difficulties, particularly in social situations.[13] For example, some autistic girls learn to maintain eye contact and suppress their discomfort to conform to social norms, or carefully 'study' the behaviours and interests of peers and mimic those in order to fit in better socially. However, maintaining this façade can be very exhausting and often puts them under an enormous amount of pressure. This, in turn, could result in anxiety, panic attacks, emotional distress and withdrawal, amongst others. The needs of autistic girls who mask their difficulties and have no accompanying learning difficulties are often not reflected in existing autism resources compared to the needs of young people with what may be considered more 'traditional' presentations and behaviours (externalized rather than internalized distress, social communication difficulties and/or accompanying language and learning difficulties).

## What causes the diagnostic bias?
### Externally vs internally expressed presentation of autism and gender
As we have already established, masking and internalizing are not restricted to girls and many autistic people, regardless of

gender, present with a high-masking, internalizing profile. In that sense, while this presentation may be more prevalent amongst girls, gender is not the only factor that we need to consider. We also need to think about the variety of factors that may mean autistic girls are more likely to go undetected, even if their profile of needs is similar to that of boys, such as any preconceived ideas we may hold about what constitutes 'typical' behaviour in boys or girls. For example, consider the case studies below:

### MALAKAI

Malakai is 10 years old and school staff describe him as a 'bright' boy who works at or above age-related expectations in all subjects. Malakai comes across as very shy and, while he has a small group of friends at school, he appears to find 'playground dynamics' overwhelming. While he displays no signs of distress in school, he has told his parents that he 'hates' being in school and finds leaving the house every morning difficult. Malakai's quietness and very limited interaction with his peers immediately stood out as unusual to school staff and he was referred to the school's educational psychologist who then recommended a neurodevelopmental assessment.

### AVA

Ava is 10 years old; her parents reported having longstanding difficulties managing her emotional needs at home; however, none of those difficulties were ever observed at school. Ava is a very capable student academically, but she is generally shy in class and speaks in a very quiet voice;

she has one close friend at school and staff have observed that she becomes tearful if her friend is absent. Apart from that, Ava presents as very well-behaved and always follows the teacher's instructions. When she goes home, however, she is 'like a different child' – her parents report that she is chatty and energetic, and regularly becomes very dysregulated over what others may see as minor issues. In those instances, Ava appears unable to control her own reactions – she shouts and throws objects in frustration, which then leaves her very exhausted. Ava appears to be deeply embarrassed after those episodes and does not want to talk about them. School staff are struggling to imagine how Ava can present so differently at home and at school, and query whether her parents might need parenting support, which made Ava's parents feel judged and misunderstood.

Malakai and Ava present in a very similar way at school; however, Malakai's needs were picked up earlier, likely because his presentation didn't conform to the gender stereotype of what a boy 'should' supposedly do and be like, i.e., boisterous, energetic and sociable. In contrast, Ava's presentation is arguably perceived as less 'out-of-the-ordinary', and her underlying anxiety is seen as 'shyness'. It is also important to consider that anxiety can be (wrongly) perceived as a 'female' trait and, as such, be dismissed as less serious or concerning when observed in a girl – or not be recognized at all in a boy, especially if externally expressed, when it may come across as anger. We need to challenge and examine any preconceived ideas we may have about what anxiety may look like – is the picture that automatically appears in our minds one of a shy, timid child sitting in the corner and looking scared? While this may reflect what anxiety looks like for some children, for others, their anxiety may be expressed through disengagement, reluctance to complete work or a strong aversive response against the anxiety-provoking situation (i.e., becoming very angry at school or doing something that will send the child out of the classroom, which may be overwhelming, to a quieter area). In this instance, the child's behaviour may instead be labelled 'disruptive' and 'challenging' and the link to anxiety – the recognition that the behaviour is, in fact, an anxiety response – may be missed altogether.

## Lack of understanding of what autism may look like in girls and women on the 'ground level'

I think the lack of information and awareness of how autism can present in females or the clues to indicate masked autism played a huge role in my discovery and diagnosis not happening until I was 46.

*AA, autistic woman*

For a child or a young person to have their needs recognized and/or obtain a diagnosis, should they wish so, usually an adult – a family member, teacher or another professional – needs to recognize their needs or differences. However, considering the widely prevalent, simplistic stereotypes surrounding autism, recognizing internalized or masked autism in any child, and particularly in girls, is likely to be a challenge. For many, the process may take several years and the young person might accumulate a number of other diagnoses in the meantime, depending on which sign of distress becomes most noticeable (e.g., anxiety, low mood, difficulty regulating emotions due to being overwhelmed). In other cases, the child's autism and needs could be missed altogether, especially if they are academically strong and appear to be 'doing well', and they might not recognize that they are autistic until adulthood.

---

I apparently had a gifted diagnosis as a child. I never felt it fit, as there were (and still are) so many things I am terrible at! Although I have an excellent memory and quick processing, it can take me time to translate thoughts/feelings into words. I also seem to lack the critical thinking I associate with giftedness, as I tend to believe people's assertions and can be naive as a result.

Teachers accommodated to some degree for my giftedness but expected me to just know how to organize ideas, write essays, break down projects and manage my time. Supports with these skills would have been helpful and removed a lot of the guesswork. No one taught me how to study and I relied on my exceptional memory until university when there was too much content to memorize. They also failed to recognize my vulnerability, seating me with peers who bullied me and not intervening when I was not given a Kris Kringle gift (each classmate buys a gift for another), when I was called on to start the dance with another nerdy student as a joke, and other events that were excruciatingly painful and isolating.

*KD, autistic woman*

I was first assessed for autism as a young child, and although I clearly displayed a lot of autistic traits, I ended up being diagnosed with a language disorder as I had delayed speech too. I was also masking at a very young age and I believe that the professionals did not pick up on this. It wasn't until I got to adulthood and I was struggling massively that I started to question if I was autistic, and then did my own research. After doing this research and finding out more about autistic women and girls, I knew my original diagnosis was wrong, and that I needed to be reassessed as an adult.

I had to go to a specialist diagnostician who had expertise in autistic women and girls. I genuinely feel that if I wasn't masking or was a boy, I would have got the right diagnosis a lot earlier.

*SB, autistic woman*

---

## WHAT DOES THE RESEARCH SAY ABOUT EDUCATORS' ABILITY TO RECOGNIZE AUTISM IN GIRLS?

---

Teachers had no clue; they just saw me as a shy child. As I wasn't being disruptive they didn't care and were not the allies I needed to survive school. I think so much has to change within our schools to meet many autistic people's needs. Outside of big changes within the school system (which is needed alongside adaptations), empathy is what teachers can offer. Having a teacher being prepared to listen in a non-judgemental way is what I really needed, and a teacher to advocate on my behalf when things didn't go well.

*SB, autistic woman*

Some teachers did understand my needs, but I think because I wasn't diagnosed at any point during my school journey, except for the last four months of A Levels, it was more they met me on a needs-based level rather than a label-based level. They didn't know why I was different, or what I needed support with, instead, they focused on bringing in the things that were important to me, and on treating me with empathy and kindness.

*SO, autistic woman*

---

A study published in 2020 sheds some light on this important question. A team of researchers carried out a study with 289 primary school teachers, trainee teachers and teaching assistants in the UK in an attempt to better understand how gender and the different autism presentations affect educators' perceptions.[14] The researchers presented the educators with four case studies: one of a child with what the researchers called the 'male autism phenotype' – or what is referred to as 'externalized' or 'unmasked' autism in this book; the second one with the 'female autism phenotype' – or the 'internalized' or 'masked' profile more commonly observed in girls; and they also included two 'distraction' case studies of children with separation anxiety and Attention Deficit Hyperactivity Disorder (ADHD), which were introduced so that it was not obvious to the participants that the study was focused on identifying autism.

The *only* aspect of the vignettes the researchers changed between participants was gender – so, while all participants were given both the internalizing and externalizing autism case studies, the gender of the fictional child varied. For example, the externalized presentation of autism case study could be either 'Jack' or 'Chloe', and the internalized autism case study could be either 'Jack' or 'Chloe'. The 'distractor' vignettes' genders were randomized too. The participants were asked to indicate how likely they thought each child was to have autism, ADHD, 'an anxiety disorder' or 'a behaviour disorder'. The educators were also asked to indicate how likely they were to seek additional support for each child 1) within the school, 2) from an educational psychologist and 3) from a medical or mental health professional.

Their findings were fascinating and tell us more about several important areas:

- *Role of popular perceptions of autism:* what the researchers referred to as the 'female presentation', i.e., internalized autism, is generally less recognized as autism than the 'male presentation', i.e., externalized or unmasked autism, in all children, regardless of gender.

- *Role of gender stereotypes:* The gender of the child made the internalized presentation even more difficult to recognize. The characteristics of the externalized presentation were judged as being 70% likely to indicate autism regardless of the child's gender. The internalized presentation was somewhat less likely to be recognized when it was labelled with a boy's name, Jack. But the perceived likelihood that it was reflective of autism dropped to 55% when the same internalized presentation was given a girl's name, Chloe. So, if two children presented in an identical way, the girl would be at a disadvantage as her difficulties would be less likely to be identified.

- The study also indicated that there was a gap between recognizing the symptoms and seeking support from an educational psychologist or a mental health professional. Participants said they were more likely to refer the child for support when the description was given a boy's name than a girl's – *regardless of the presentation.* But for girls with an internalized presentation, the percentage dropped even further. Girls are thus at a higher risk of not receiving support for their needs – because autistic girls in general are less likely to be recognized than boys with an identical presentation, but also because many girls tend to have a particular presentation that is, in itself, under-recognized by professionals.

- Educators were more likely to refer girls with the 'male presentation' (i.e., externalized or unmasked presentation) than those with the 'female' or masked presentation, but also less likely to refer boys with the 'male presentation' than with the 'female', because both types of children deviate from what is socially expected of them. In this way, even some autistic boys can end up undiagnosed because of simplistic gender stereo-types, as their presentation could be taken as more 'gender-appropriate'.

- We do also need to consider that the study is likely to significantly over-estimate the rates of recognizing autism and requesting help for boys and girls alike, as the participants were explicitly told to look for signs of additional needs – which, in real-world classrooms of 20 children or more, they may be less likely to do that pro-actively. It can be argued that, in the 'real world', many of those children's needs may simply go undetected.

## Diagnostic process and assessment tools

Another very important factor to consider is the inherent bias in the 'gold standard', most commonly used autism assessment tools. Our understanding of what autism is has developed over time – and is still evolving. Historically, autism was seen as a 'male' condition, with a very specific set of characteristics; the most outwardly visible presentations and behaviours became codified in the diagnostic criteria (e.g., repetitive motor movements; 'highly restricted, fixated interests'; lack of reciprocity in the context of social communication). However, we have only recently started to recognize that this is just one way of being autistic and that there are other, more subtle and internalizing expressions of autism. Those remained largely undetected and, considering that the internalizing presentation is more common in girls and women, they, too, were largely left out of the autism research and literature. This, in turn, meant that the key diagnostic assessments were developed with the 'male' and externalizing presentation of autism in mind, leading to a self-perpetuating cycle of under-recognition and under-diagnosis (see Figure 1.2).

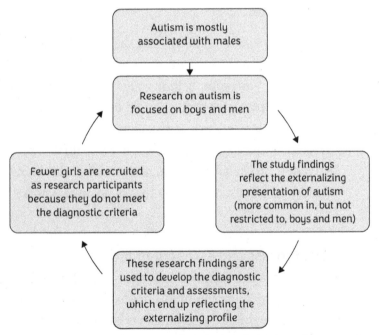

*Figure 1.2: The cycle of under-representation of girls in autism research*

One example of this is 'repetitive and stereotypical behaviours', which have been included as indicative of autism in the *Diagnostic and Statistical Manual of Mental Disorders, Fifth Edition* (DSM-5).[15] However, research has shown that girls tend to exhibit fewer repetitive behaviours than boys, and it is also possible that such behaviours are different in nature than the boys', making them harder to recognize.[16,17] Another criterion is special interests – autistic boys are stereotypically presented as being intensely interested in dinosaurs or trains, and while this can also be observed in girls, their special interests also tend to be more similar to those of their neurotypical peers, such as books, dolls, specific actors, musicians or TV programmes. It is the intensity and focus of the special interest, rather than the interest itself, that needs to be considered (as we will discuss in more detail in the next section). Because the diagnostic criteria are not attuned to such gender differences in presentation, some autistic girls fall below the diagnostic threshold and are left undiagnosed or misdiagnosed.

Further bias could be introduced not just in the formulation of diagnostic criteria and thresholds, but in parents and clinicians' use of assessments and diagnostic tools. Some diagnostic tools, such as the Autism Diagnostic Interview – Revised (ADI-R), rely on the parents' reports of their child's presentation. Those, however, could be influenced by the prevalent gender norms for children's behaviour. Other assessments can be dependent on the practitioner's experience of working with autistic girls and their understanding of the variety of ways in which autism can present in women. This degree of personal discretion could add a layer of bias, but it could also help to correct it even when the diagnostic criteria have not yet been updated to reflect the more internalizing presentation. For example, the practitioner doing the assessment can reach the conclusion that an autism diagnosis is warranted even when the child technically falls below the Autism Diagnostic Observation Schedule's (ADOS) diagnostic threshold. A recent study by Stroth and colleagues[18] found that practitioners do this slightly more often for girls (18.6%) than for boys (13.5%), which could indicate that when making diagnostic decisions about autistic girls and women, practitioners are sometimes having to rely on relevant information which is not present in the ADOS.

## Special interests may be 'gender-conforming' or expressed differently and go undetected

---

*Is she mute?* No, she's just shy. (She can talk at home. She just needs to speak up more at school.) *What about obsessions? Special interests?* Not really. (As the dolls lined-up and toy pony collections grew.) The diagnoses for anxiety and depression came later. Observable, tick-offable. But the way it felt when I had the last sparkle pony in a set? The click, the relief, the joy? That feeling of oneness, like all-is-right in the world? They couldn't see that. They couldn't see how hard I worked to be liked, to be like them. I turned myself inside out to be someone else, and I've paid the price ever since.

*Jolene Stockman, autistic*

---

Much of the public discourse around autism, as well as the way autistic people are portrayed in popular culture, centres around the niche and 'eccentric' nature of the special interests autistic people are supposed to have. The *unusualness* of the interest is typically emphasized as its key, defining feature.

Because of these prevalent stereotypes, girls' special interests may be seen as too 'conventional' to fit that inaccurate label – especially if their interests are also gender-conforming. For example, based on the popular representation of autistic special interests, we may expect that girls will have an intense interest in trains, dinosaurs and machines; while some may indeed fall into that category, others' interests may not be particularly unusual or 'niche' (e.g., reading, fashion, one particular TV programme/character/actor/musician/artist) but just as intense and focused. Even researching autism itself can become a special interest for some autistic people. It is, therefore, important that we reconsider our expectations when it comes to special interests and focus on the *intensity* of the interest rather than on its specific nature.

---

I was a huge reader, which of course links to autistic hyperlexia, but I was reading books way beyond my years at extreme rates. I think this wasn't seen as a special interest because it could just be seen as a hobby and part of me being so-called 'gifted and talented', and fiction reading is seen as a hobby lots of young girls have.

*Charli Clement, autistic non-binary person*

My special interests around reading, pop music, films and TV would all be deemed 'normal'. They all offered me sensory soothing, escapism from interacting with other people and education into how people interacted and developed relationships – all areas that I struggled with.

*AA, autistic woman*

A lot of my interests were related to TV shows or films (and characters within them). I also had interests in games that are perceived as more feminine, so they didn't stand out, and as a result nobody connected the dots that the level of interest I had in them was due to my autism.

*SB, autistic woman*

I think it [the diagnosis] was delayed because I'm a woman, I don't think it was recognized earlier because my special interests weren't the things that people expected them to be. I didn't fit the stereotype at the time that I was growing up so I was missed.

My special interests were always in books, or reading, crafting, categorizing information, and things that were slightly girly, but would always mean I was called a tomboy.

*SO, autistic woman*

It is also important to consider how conventional or even socially desirable special interests, such as reading, going to the theatre or watching movies/social media videos, can potentially mask some autistic girls' social communication differences. All of these activities are generally self-directed and solitary in nature, but are not immediately flagged as such – while going to the theatre or watching a film may appear to be a social activity at first glance, it involves sitting quietly for a number of hours in a highly structured way and in a relatively predictable environment. That is not to say that a preference for these activities is in any way socially dysfunctional or that autistic people should be 'pushed' towards more interactive activities and interests, which could be very harmful. Rather, it is important to consider day-to-day behaviours and preferences through the wider lens of neurodivergence.

Failure to do so may lead to delayed diagnosis and lack of recognition as those behaviours, interests and differences are often seen through a simplistic lens and are conceptualized as either 'good' or 'bad' – e.g., not socializing with peers is 'bad'; sitting quietly, being studious and reading books is 'good'. Therefore, the former is often considered a concerning presentation and a sign that something must be wrong, whereas the latter is not detected as a potential sign of neurodivergence. This highlights why special interests and the child's broader presentation should not be considered solely in terms of the impact they may have on those around them; rather, we need to consider, and ask, how those activities are experienced by the individual.

## Absence of language difficulties and learning disabilities (sometimes also referred to as 'intellectual disability')

Autistic girls with no accompanying language difficulties or learning disabilities – those who are likely to be working broadly within or even above age-related expectations academically – are at a particularly high risk of 'slipping through the net'. When a child has significant learning-related difficulties, those are usually easier to spot by others and, in most cases, the child would require additional support and their learning would need to be suitably differentiated. Once again, this is an example of how autistic people's needs are detected as such when they have a direct impact on those around them, but when this is not the case and the impact of those difficulties is primarily internal, they may not be spotted for a very long time – or until a crisis point is reached.

## Reaching a crisis point: Complications due to unrecognized needs

I was formally diagnosed during my admission to a CAMHS psychiatric unit after falling into crisis. I was suspected autistic for a couple of months before my admission when my mental health crisis had begun with what professionals have since suspected was a reaction to being unable to mask any longer: a burnout manifesting in panic attacks and meltdowns.

We shouldn't have to fall into crisis in order for someone to realize we are autistic, but this is an extremely common story. I think being assigned female at birth contributed significantly to this – ultimately, I can look back and see so many obvious traits across my childhood before that point, but I was just seen as quirky, quiet, a bit weird, but so academic that nobody really noticed anything.

*Charli Clement, autistic non-binary person*

Autistic girls' needs often become more apparent towards the later stages of primary school or as they start secondary school. The likely reasons for this are complex. First, the transition to secondary school is usually characterized by increasingly more complex social dynamics and relationships, which are no longer based around doing activities and playing games together, but around conversations. It is possible that the internalized profile isn't recognized in the primary school years because of masking, but it is also possible that for some autistic people this was a time when their needs were actually being met, at least partially, as they had predictability and consistency, and the social relationships were easier to navigate. Their needs, therefore, may go unnoticed for a very long time, until they reach a breaking point, often due to being overwhelmed by a combination of increased environmental demands and insufficient or no support and adaptations due to unrecognized needs. This, in turn, could lead to a cycle of assessments that are initially focused on the presenting problem – such as the autistic young woman's extreme distress, anxiety, panic attacks or inability to attend school, which, while very real in their impact on her wellbeing, are the end result, rather than the root cause, of her difficulties. As such, many autistic young women can accumulate a range of diagnoses that, at best, only partially capture their needs, before autism is even considered.

While views on the usefulness of diagnosis vary and the question of whether to seek a formal diagnosis, especially in adulthood, is a deeply personal choice, many services and funding sources, particularly during the school years, do require a diagnosis. Similarly, we do still live in a society and within systems where a diagnosis is often synonymous with recognition of needs. Therefore, not having those needs recognized at an early stage, so that the necessary support and adaptations can be put in place in a preventative manner, could further exacerbate any difficulties already experienced by autistic young women.

It is also important to consider that the likelihood of receiving an autism diagnosis declines sharply after the age of 20, meaning that many young people whose needs were not recognized while they were of school age may never be formally recognized. A 2023 study of autism diagnosis rates across the lifespan based on GP practice records in England highlights a worrying trend – both men and women are significantly less likely to be diagnosed in their 20s compared to adolescence and that likelihood goes down further as they age.[19] This decline is very sharp already for people in their 20s, which further highlights the importance of recognizing autistic young people's needs when they are of school age and providing efficient assessment pathways for adults. It is also worth considering that access to free adult assessment services can vary considerably, and some adults may feel like they have little choice but to seek a private assessment, likely at a considerable cost:

I was able to find a clinic and pay out of pocket for an assessment. I never shared my suspicions of being autistic with my family doctor because I feared not being believed. It was only because I found a clinic of neurodivergent diagnosticians that I felt like my concerns would be taken seriously and that perhaps they would understand I can't do ratings scales for the life of me. Because they allowed online booking, I eventually mustered up the courage and executive functioning spoons to start the process. From there, I went in armed with a 21-page document charting my traits over my lifespan into a variety of categories. It was almost 7000 words! I was assured that alone was a good sign I was autistic.

*KD, autistic woman*

It is also important to consider that while being diagnosed in adulthood can be a positive and life-affirming experience for many autistic people, finding an experienced and suitably trained diagnostician can be difficult to navigate; however, if the assessment is not handled by the diagnostician with the care and sensitivity it deserves, the process can result in distress that could have otherwise been avoided:

---

I didn't even attempt to explore autism with a general practitioner. Having first found a clinical psychologist to help our son formally identify his autism, I asked her for a recommendation for a clinical psychologist who works with late discovered women to diagnose autism. I went with a clinical psychologist who I felt comfortable to talk to on Zoom (it was during the pandemic) and who I knew would be thorough.

I was ill prepared for how traumatic I found the assessment process. In particular I found the aspect of gathering childhood development evidence from my mum to be the most difficult. The process I was advised to follow should have been more carefully considered for its traumatic impact.

I had to send my mum an extensive questionnaire for her to consider the questions. My mum wanted to break the questions down into three chunks. I then had to interview her on the telephone, write down her responses and then type them up for the clinical psychologist.

To hear, note and then see the words in black and white on a screen like 'We always knew you were different', 'You have an inappropriate laugh' and 'You wouldn't share your things, which was a problem for your brother and your cousins' was deeply shaming and troublesome when I was dealing with the unravelling of my entire life through a new lens.

I then received my official report which was difficult to decipher in its heavy psychology speak and I had to deal with the residual difficult emotions and thoughts without any kind of support. I now understand there are many neuro-inclusive adult assessments which are a much more therapeutic

experience which I would heavily encourage any adult exploring an autism diagnosis to pursue. I wouldn't want anyone to
go through the process I did.

*AA, autistic woman*

## Social media and diagnosis

In recent years, the move to video-based social media plat-
forms such as TikTok has led to the popularity of mental health
and neurodiversity-related content – short explanatory clips
that focus on identifying key characteristics of conditions such
as depression and anxiety, as well as videos focused on autism
and ADHD. This has led to numerous newspaper headlines
warning of the dangers of young people supposedly 'self-diag-
nosing on TikTok', such as *The Telegraph* and *The Independent*
articles below:

'Fears teenagers self-diagnose autism and ADHD using
TikTok'[20]

'Inside TikTok's damaging self-diagnosis trend'[21]

The Plummer article also asks, 'How did we reach a world in
which young people are outsourcing their diagnoses to their
phones?'

There certainly are many examples of misconceptions or
overly simplistic and incomplete information on social media;
those can undoubtedly be very harmful, and safety should, of
course, always come first. Similarly, while it may be tempting
to try to summarize a broad range of characteristics that are
supposedly indicators of certain conditions, many of those
have overlapping traits. Attempting to neatly summarize
them and produce a list of 'symptoms' or 'signs' is bound to

be reductionist and can result in wrong or overly simplistic ideas of what certain conditions might entail.

However, social media does remain a powerful platform and source of information for many people, including, and perhaps particularly, for young people. If professionals are unwilling to engage with the content that many young people are exposed to, this would leave no space for discussions and, even more importantly, for addressing and challenging the misconceptions that may be perpetuated. It is also important to acknowledge that social media does provide a platform for voices that have historically been denied one, such as actually autistic women sharing their experiences, and those can be powerful influencers of change. Rather than judging young people for supposedly 'diagnosing themselves on TikTok', it would be much more helpful to use that as a discussion starter and an opportunity to directly address any misconceptions and recommend suitable alternative resources, while also gaining an understanding of how the young person experiences the world.

It is also worth emphasizing that this is a much more complex issue than young people choosing to 'diagnose' themselves on social media. This narrative appears to present a version of reality where access to diagnostic services is readily, easily and freely available to all, and some people choose to opt out of this supposedly accessible service and instead resort to watching videos on social media. In my experience, the reality is much more complicated and nuanced than that. On the one hand, as many people who have tried to access a diagnostic assessment in the UK will be able to attest, the waiting list for those can be very long, meaning that those seeking a diagnosis or waiting for an assessment often have no support or explanation for their differences and difficulties. Of course, the answer to this is not going to be seeking a diagnosis on social media; however, we do also need to question whether this is what is *actually* happening. Anecdotally, none of the young people I have known personally or professionally go on social media with the explicit intention to self-diagnose through watching videos on their phones – rather, they came across content that made sense to them and gave them an explanation for experiences, differences and difficulties they had not been able to fully make sense of previously. That is not to diminish the very real issues with unregulated content on social media that is not fact-checked and could contain wrong, misleading or harmful information – safety should always come first. However, mocking those who have come across content that resonated with their experiences on social media or reducing this to a desire to self-diagnose through their phones is not the answer either. Rather, we need to ensure that public services that provide diagnostic assessments and post-diagnostic support are available and sufficiently funded, and that young people who are questioning whether they may be autistic can be provided with accurate information and opportunities to dispel any misconceptions they may have come across, without fear of judgement.

# CHAPTER 2

# School and Education

To put it brutally, school was hell. Masking was a fear response to the environment I was in to try and get through the day unnoticed. The amount of change during the school day (particularly secondary school) was too much due to executive dysfunction. Sensory-wise, being in large schools was difficult. Also, having social differences also meant I was an easy target for bullies, and I did not have the ability to stand up for myself at the time. Undoubtedly being autistic impacted my school experiences, and being subjected to that place over such a long period of time has left me traumatized.

*SB, autistic woman*

Navigating the complex and often confusing world of school – and the education system more broadly – can be an overwhelming process for many autistic people, regardless of gender. While some may find sanctuary in the structure, routine and relative predictability of the school day, others find the social aspects of school – friendship dynamics, managing arguments, disagreements and unwritten social conventions – as well as the need to follow a set of sometimes very rigid rules, exceptionally challenging and stressful. These social demands tend to increase exponentially in secondary school (or even as early as the later stages of primary school), as students move away from structured play as a way of socializing, to more conversation-based interactions – about themselves, other people, relationships and personal experiences. These conversations and relationships, however, are rarely straightforward and easy to navigate – they can contain implied meaning (things that are not said explicitly but are assumed), sarcasm and irony, and saying something for the sake of figuring out how the other person might react. Based on these interactions and one's ability to engage with and respond to them, lines are drawn in terms of who belongs to the group and who doesn't. To make matters even more complicated, those criteria (i.e., what is considered desirable, interesting or popular) can change quickly. All these factors can make navigating school exceptionally challenging for autistic people.

Autistic girls who internalize their needs, differences and difficulties are at a particularly high risk of 'slipping through the net' and their needs going unnoticed. We need to remember that children and young people spend most of their time during term-time either being at school or preparing for school; school is the terrain on which most of their friendships will form and be tested, many of their first interactions with authority will play out, and their capacity for work and creativity will expand or be hindered, if their needs are not fully understood. School is, therefore, a key aspect of their lives – if their needs are understood and supported appropriately, school can become an important source of positivity, acceptance and success. If, however, their needs are not recognized and supported, the implications are likely to go far beyond the school gates and affect multiple aspects of their life – from education and employment prospects to their mental health and social relationships. 'Getting it right' for autistic girls at school is of critical importance – and this requires a *proactive*, rather than a *reactive*, approach. Only noticing and responding to autistic girls' needs when they have reached a crisis point and are distressed or no longer able to attend school isn't good enough. If we truly want autistic girls to thrive in education, we need to commit to identifying their needs much sooner, even in girls who are not unsettled or distressed. A key part of this process is learning to recognize some of the main areas of difficulty autistic girls may find challenging in school.

## 'Keeping it all in' at school

We're not always the ones kicking and thrashing. Sometimes we're quiet and compliant. Hard to spot, easy to teach. When I was ten, my school had special badges for science, maths and art. The badges were cute and shiny. Deliciously collectible. And best of all? I could earn them by completing extension projects outside of school hours. Challenging, satisfying work, and the bonus of being rewarded with a treasure. I completed them all. I loved the work. Hours of reading, writing, colouring. But I never handed the projects in. I never got my badges. Because the badges were presented on stage. At assembly. In front of the whole school. The school saw that as recognition, I saw it as punishment. It was less energy to acquiesce. Less energy to stay small, stay hidden. I wish someone had seen me.

*Jolene Stockman, autistic*

As we have already established, it is common for autistic girls to mask or camouflage their difficulties and differences – this can be a laborious and exhausting process with a considerable impact on their mental health and wellbeing that can include the following (amongst many others – this is far from an exhaustive list).

Autistic girls may:

- engage in some social activities alongside peers but be on the periphery of the group and following rather than initiating interaction, games or conversations

- closely observe how other young people talk, behave, dress and what their interests are – and try to mimic this in order to 'fit in'

- rehearse conversations and have scripts for specific situations

- make eye contact even if that feels counterintuitive or stressful

- present as very quiet in class and try to 'blend in' so as not to attract attention

- carefully study films, YouTube videos or interviews for cues and ideas for different ways of conducting themselves socially

- become very focused on being a 'good student' or someone who does not 'get into trouble', and any minor perceived deviation from this (i.e., being 'told off' by the teacher or receiving a detention) can result in extreme anxiety and distress

- present as calm and very well-behaved in school but become dysregulated and exhausted as soon as they return home.

It is even easier for some autistic girls' already hidden needs to be missed in an environment as busy as a school where many children and young people will externalize their difficulties, making them harder to ignore, and where opportunities for regular staff training may be limited. In that context, even well-meaning professionals can wrongly assume that lack of obvious externalizing behaviours means lack of significant need, as illustrated in Figure 2.1.

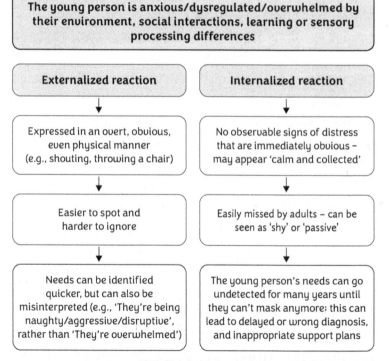

*Figure 2.1: Differences between externalized and internalized expressions of distress*

We also need to consider how autistic girls' needs may change considerably in secondary school. Primary schools tend to be smaller scale environments that provide more consistency over the course of the school day – children tend to stay in the same classroom, with the same teacher and group of children, over the course of the day. It is, therefore, not unusual for autistic girls, and, indeed, autistic young people regardless of gender, to present as more 'settled' at this stage of their education and for primary school staff to have nothing significant to report in terms of concerns to the young person's secondary school. In some cases, autistic young women's parents may have been reporting concerns about their daughter's presentation at home – high anxiety levels, reluctance to go to school in the morning, extreme distress and 'meltdowns' on Sunday evenings. However, those may have been seen as a 'home issue' and not taken with the seriousness a significant discrepancy in presentation between home and school should be treated.

Often, this is a sign that the child is masking or internalizing their difficulties at school, where their anxiety levels are likely to be very high, and externalizing, or unmasking, in the safer environment of the home. Maintaining this facade at school is not sustainable long-term and the changes and increased demands of secondary schools or the later stages of primary school may, in turn, mean that the young person is no longer able to mask their difficulties at school. It is often at this point that school staff who may have previously had no concerns start to observe very similar difficulties to the ones reported by the parents at home. This is often a sign that the young person has reached a crisis point and that they are no longer coping. While this certainly does not mean that intervening at this point would be futile – far from it – a preventative approach may have been more impactful and could have spared the young person considerable distress. This is why it is fundamentally important that the views of both autistic young people and their parents are sought routinely and, even more importantly, listened to and taken seriously.

## Traditional 'behaviour management' strategies and anxiety

Many school behaviour policies and behaviour management strategies are based on punishment and reward (e.g., behaviour charts where desirable behaviours are rewarded and undesirable ones lead to consequences; detentions and fixed-term exclusions; 100% attendance awards). While this may be an effective way of disciplining some students without undue effect on their mental health, it is important to recognize that those may be a major source of distress for autistic people that could elevate their anxiety levels at school exponentially.

For example, let's consider how detentions, or the fear of detentions and similar consequences, can affect an autistic girl who internalizes her anxiety. First, she may become fixated on the implications of the detention, which is a deviation from her usual routine that can also be highly humiliating as other students are usually aware of it and the circumstances around it. Additionally, a detention can challenge the autistic young woman's securely established self-perception as a good student, or as a student who 'doesn't get in trouble'. This can lead to a level of anxiety and distress that school staff may not be able to fully appreciate if applying neurotypical standards based on their experiences with non-autistic students.

We all have a duty to ensure that autistic people are treated in an equitable way – and this does not necessarily mean being treated in the exact same way as everyone else. Arguing that 'consequences must be the same for everyone' in the interest of equality and consistency misses a very important point – the same punishment can have very different, and much more severe, consequences for an autistic child compared to neurotypical children. Similarly, taking an inflexible 'The rules are the rules, and they apply to everyone equally' position fails to acknowledge the very real need for personalized differentiation for autistic young people not just in the classroom, but in all aspects of school life. It is also worth considering that, if an autistic young person said this very statement, it would, in all likelihood, be used as supporting evidence for their supposed lack of flexibility and rigidity of mind. It is only fair, then, that professionals and institutions should hold themselves to the same standard and proactively identify areas of policy and practice that do not meet the needs of the people they are meant to support. A good policy should be flexible and evolve over time, and with the changing profile of need at the school, it should not be treated as a natural law that cannot be amended. Of course, that is not to say that schools should adopt an anarchistic approach with no rules or expectations; rather, it is important to consider neurodivergent pupils' needs routinely and tailor the school's policies and behaviour management strategies accordingly, for a truly inclusive and equitable learning environment.

## Transitions

I particularly struggled at secondary school. I was bullied throughout my time there and was regularly off sick as the overwhelming demands and fear of being picked on were too much for me to cope with. I struggled with friendships a great deal. I really loved English, music and drama but would be terrified of having to perform to the whole class, year or school. Whilst I loved the rehearsals and learning, I was never, ever able to carry it through to be present for the final performance – I was always off sick. A repeated theme in my school reports is that I 'needed to believe in myself'; 'participate in classroom discussion and not be afraid to speak out and share my ideas'; 'needs more self-confidence'.

*AA, autistic woman*

Transitions, in all their forms, can be a considerable challenge for autistic young people, and particularly for those who mask their difficulties. The transition from primary to secondary school can pose its own unique set of challenges, such as having to navigate a much larger physical environment, making new friendships and managing (or trying to manage) other people's perception of you, an overall noisier and busier environment, as well as becoming the youngest and newest members of the school community – as opposed to being among the oldest in primary school. These are all major readjustments for any child; however, they can be particularly unsettling for autistic young people who are more likely to find changes difficult to navigate. This is not the only major transition young people encounter in education – transitions take place regularly, on a yearly, termly, weekly and even daily basis, such as:

- transitions from the summer holidays to the new academic year; from term time to half-term; from spending time at home over the Christmas and Easter breaks to returning to school for the new term

- transitions during the day:

  - from home to school, including transport changes if travelling by public transport

  - from one classroom to another – those are particularly frequent in secondary schools

  - from one teacher, teaching style and set of expectations to another – this can also affect other factors such as the noise levels in the classroom

  - in-class transitions – from one activity to another or from individual work to group work

  - from unstructured times (e.g., playtime/breaks and lunchtime) to structured learning

  - from PE/swimming to classroom-based learning and vice versa.

This highlights how many changes and transitions, which may not even register as such for neurotypical people, are prevalent over the course of the school day. While many of these changes may be inevitable, the associated distress that many autistic people experience as a result isn't. Careful, individualized transition planning and support – such as a key adult to offer support and accompany the young person during transition times – can be an important step in terms of both preventing further escalation of needs and demonstrating the school's commitment and care for the young person's wellbeing.

## Unstructured times and changes to routine

While most people benefit from having a degree of order and predictability to their day, regularity and routines are vital for many autistic people's very sense of stability and calm in their lives. Autistic people can be very sensitive to any disruptions of routines and can experience them as profoundly unsettling and distressing.

These do not have to be just 'formally' established or regimented routines, such as timetables and planned activities with a clear beginning, middle and end. Daily habits that other people may not recognize as routines (e.g., which route to take to school, which side of the road to walk on) can become instrumental in maintaining a sense of calm and predictability, which can be soothing and give the autistic person a sense of control and safety. It is, therefore, important to remember that it is not up to the adults, or neurotypical people in general, to decide what is a 'legitimate' routine – i.e., which ones can be ignored, and which ones should be 'respected' or accommodated. A routine is anything that the child perceives as a routine.

The disruption or lack of a routine can be experienced by many autistic people as profoundly unsettling and disorienting. This is not equivalent to the kind of minor inconvenience that a neurotypical person might experience, and they should not be told to simply 'get on with it' because 'changes happen in life'. Many autistic people cannot do that as easily. In fact, the experience is often so profoundly uncomfortable and unsettling that it can cause extreme distress. In such cases, the response of the professionals and other adults in the autistic young person's life is going to be essential in helping to contain that distress. People unfamiliar with the difficulties that autistic people experience around loss of structure can fall back on harmful gender stereotypes to dismiss or downplay the distress experienced by autistic girls by branding them 'emotional', 'difficult' or 'hysterical'. This could result in a cycle of escalation, where the child's distress increases, which is then seen as confirmation of her 'unreasonableness', and the root cause of her distress – the disrupted routine – remains unaddressed, and possibly even unidentified.

While the typical school day may seem, at least at first glance, to be highly structured, this is far from the case in reality. It is, by design, interrupted by pockets of unstructured time, each with its own set of potential challenges. For example, whereas social interactions during lessons are mostly constrained and managed by the teacher and the demands of the learning, socialization during break times is much more open-ended and unpredictable. For many children, this will provide some welcome respite and freedom, but for autistic children the lack of structure and clear parameters can be confusing, stressful and hard to navigate. They might experience a feeling similar to being pushed onto a theatre stage in front of a large audience, mid-performance, without a script. Lunch times pose very similar challenges with the added potential for sensory overload – the smells and noises in the dinner hall, combined with the smells, texture and taste of the food.

Other disruptions to school routine may not be registered as such by the adults because they appear to be 'fun' and 'enjoyable' on the surface. Those include birthday celebrations, sports days, PE lessons with the associated changes before and after, school performances, presentations and 'wear your own clothes to school' days. While it is not suggested that these will be experienced as stressful by all autistic people, we need to acknowledge that (1) they are a deviation from the usual routine, and (2) they require the performance of excitement and enjoyment in order to fit in. This can be exhausting and overwhelming, particularly for autistic young people who mask and internalize their difficulties, such as many autistic girls. The pressure to present as though they are enjoying something that they are, in fact, finding overwhelming and stressful can lead to a reluctance to attend school on days when these activities are due to take place. This can come as a surprise to the adults who, up until that point, may only have seen the child's masked presentation and, unless they know them very well, may have taken it at face value.

## The school environment and sensory processing differences

Both primary and secondary schools can be, perhaps unavoidably, busy, noisy and chaotic places. This can be demanding on a sensory processing level, but many autistic people also have difficulties with executive functioning – sustained attention, focus, working memory, organization, goal-directed behaviour.[22,23] These can pose a challenge in situations where the autistic child is required to filter out the cacophony of voices in the classroom and focus only on the words of their partner or the teacher.

Some schools have uncompromisingly strict uniform policies, and not complying with these often has consequences. This can cause a considerable amount of anxiety, as well as sensory overload, if the child finds the fit and fabric of the uniform uncomfortable. The sensory overload caused by, for example, having to always wear a blazer can be exceptionally difficult to tolerate, to an extent where it makes it impossible for the young person to engage with learning. Moreover, some autistic people who experience difficulties with interoception (conscious awareness of their own bodies and internal bodily sensations such as hunger and thirst) can experience this as a generalized sense of frustration, which can be wrongly interpreted as abruptness or defiance when it surfaces. It is also important to consider that, as autistic girls tend to get diagnosed later in life – or miss out on a diagnosis altogether – their needs may not be detected or seen through the lens of autism at this point – as such, they may miss out on support and adaptations that they would otherwise be legally entitled to.

Additionally, school rules such as those around toilet breaks can be another source of both anxiety and sensory overload. Specifically, not being allowed to freely use the toilet, particularly during menstruation, could result in intolerable sensory experiences, such as the sensation of having a soaked or leaking sanitary pad. Autistic young people who struggle with interoception may not always be able to identify the source of their sensory overload and may instead experience it as a generalized distress without an identifiable cause. As a result, they might not be able to explain to the adults in the room what is troubling them, even when asked directly. In such cases, the adults will need to get to know the child's individual sensory profile, which would require both direct work with her and liaison with the people who know her best outside of school (such as her parents).

## The social context: Challenges of navigating friendships at school

I found social situations really difficult but excelled academically. Because I was excelling academically there wasn't any cause for concern seen by teachers and those around me. I experienced a lot of bullying while at school, but again this is not something I feel teachers are well equipped to manage or step in with.

*SO, autistic woman*

As children progress through school, the social demands of the environment increase dramatically, as the nature of social interactions evolves over time. During the early stages of primary school, social interaction is often more formulaic and play-based, and it is still possible to 'blend in' by playing alongside peers or following their lead. This could allow some autistic girls to pick up the unspoken social rules and 'play the part', especially given that, on average, they tend to handle social communication and nuance somewhat better than autistic boys. However, this tends to change in the later stages of primary school and secondary school, where interpersonal relationships and conversations about mutual interests, likes, dislikes, shared experiences, and other people take precedence. Friendship dynamics become more complicated and volatile. They increasingly require a high degree of interpersonal trust and self-disclosure, attunement to nuance and subtext (which autistic people regardless of gender often struggle with), along with more complex social skills, such as those involved in managing one's reputation, triangulating between different friendship circles, curating different contextually appropriate personas, and repairing relationships. As a result, friendships can become much more intense and emotionally charged, with a higher potential for reputational damage and ostracism.

While friendships outside of school can pose the same

challenges, school friendships – and disagreements – can be uniquely intense and impactful due to the daily interactions. In that sense, in cases of arguments, there is 'nowhere to hide' from the fall-out – it can become all-encompassing and have a considerable effect on the mental health of the autistic young woman. Equally, solid, supportive friendships based on mutual trust and understanding can be a big protective and motivating factor that facilitates school attendance and school enjoyment.

---

I was bullied heavily in primary school, and unfortunately experienced the bereavement of my best friend which shaped the years to come in ways that teachers didn't really understand as they didn't understand how my brain worked. From there, I went to an all-girls grammar school as I thought going somewhere heavily academic would mean there would be more people like me – of course, I didn't understand that it wasn't my interest in academia that was what made me different. The academic pressure often meant the environment was very emotionally charged and I struggled to understand how the other girls communicated and conformed to social norms in ways I couldn't.

After I started having the panic attacks and meltdowns that caused my crisis – which originated in the school environment – and not being believed by the pastoral staff there, I ended up moving to a mainstream comprehensive secondary. I was very lucky to find a good group of friends there and I felt much more comfortable in a less pressured environment, one which took my needs seriously.

*Charli Clement, autistic non-binary person*

## Social communication differences and how they can be perceived in girls

Growing up I struggled with groups of girls – I couldn't read the invisible cues or understand why people would say one thing and do another. I could form friendships 1:1 but would be utterly perplexed when they ended – I had no idea what I'd done wrong.

I moved from Scotland to England when I was eight and this is when friendships became hugely complex and I actively started mimicking to try and blend in. The real trouble set in as a teenager when friendships and socializing became utterly bewildering and I was exhausted from trying to keep up and make myself fit. I think this is when I was publicly rejected by both girls and boys.

I found the company of boys easier, but when they started to become sexually attracted to me, I could not retain them as friends and they would be hurt by the direct communication and bluntness of my rejection; in turn they would behave cruelly to me in public.

I was often called names that stigmatized and shamed my feminine development and wronged me for my direct communication. This is when RSD [rejection sensitive dysphoria] developed strongly in me, which has troubled me and created high levels of anxiety, which I still struggle with today.

*AA, autistic woman*

While autistic girls have stronger social skills on average compared to boys,[24] many will nevertheless have social communication *differences*. For example, they may be more direct and 'to the point' than their neurotypical peers, only sharing or asking for information that is of direct relevance. This can clash with the stereotypical image of a girl as always cautiously polite and diplomatic, and can be misconstrued as being deliberately challenging or confrontational. This can go hand in hand with a particularly acute sense of justice and a need to understand the exact reasons behind rules, requests and expectations that is common in some autistic people.

---

One of my needs during school was always needing to know *why* something was the case. I couldn't understand theories and methods unless I understood the mechanisms and backgrounds to them. It was very variable as to whether teachers would help with this, because some would argue I didn't need to know and just needed to memorize for my exams. Where time was taken to help me understand, I was more likely to do well, and less likely to feel frustrated.

When I moved to comprehensive secondary, I was lucky to be quite well supported all round compared to previously, but I do wish more teachers had understood the way my anxiety manifested and particularly the circumstances that could lead to it. I had specific strategies for panic attacks, and often teachers who didn't know me would try to get involved, for example. Similarly, teachers didn't always understand that I couldn't always speak, and would get frustrated at me even if I used communication cards.

*Charli Clement, autistic non-binary person*

---

While we may not always wish to admit it, there are plenty of rules in education that make no logical sense or are based on a questionable rationale. Examples of these include rigid uniform or self-presentation rules that may apply to pupils but not to school staff. Regardless of whether we, on a personal level, accept the necessity for such rules, a dispassionate observer who wants to understand the rationale behind them would be compelled to ask logical questions: if the rationale is that pupils should look smart, the child could ask why school staff aren't required to look smart as well; if, when challenged, staff admit that there are different ways of looking smart, the child might wonder why she is required to dress the same as everyone else. These might appear to the child as arbitrary decisions made by people in authority who do not wish to abide by their own rules, provoking in the child a feeling of confusion, doubt or indignation at the perceived injustice. The questioning is thus not intended to provoke or to annoy, but merely to make sense; nevertheless, it is not uncommon for adults to misconstrue the child's behaviour as obstructive or 'persistently defiant'.

## School attendance difficulties

We are going to explore school distress or anxiety (which can culminate in the so-called 'emotionally based school non-attendance') in a lot more depth in Chapter 5, alongside key concepts such as *autistic burnout*. However, it is worth saying at this point that, in light of the many challenges autistic young women with a masked, internalizing presentation face in the educational system, many reach a breaking point when they are no longer able to sustain the daily masking required to function in school and social contexts. Internalizing or camouflaging their needs and differences is a laborious and exhausting process, and some young women become burnt out and completely overwhelmed and exhausted. It is important to emphasize that this is *not* wilful disengagement or unwillingness to attend school – hence why the loaded term 'school refusal' is not appropriate in this context. This also highlights the very real risks and implications of the unmet and poorly recognized needs of autistic women in education – once a crisis point has been reached, interventions usually need to be more intensive, both for the young person and their family, and in terms of the resources and expertise required by school staff and other professionals. Identifying autistic girls' needs early, so that timely and preventative support can be put in place, should always be a priority. We will consider how school anxiety relates to the broader mental health needs of autistic girls and young women in Chapter 5.

## The problematic concept of 'resilience'

Resilience refers to the ability to 'bounce back' after encountering a challenge, a difficult event or adversity.[25] The concept seems to have taken on a life of its own in recent years when applied to educational contexts, where schools have been encouraged to develop pupils' resilience in order to improve their outcomes.[26] While exploring what factors facilitate quicker recovery and better outcomes in some children who have experienced adverse life events is a worthwhile initiative, taking the concept of 'resilience' too literally or uncritically can have very different implications. Specifically, individuals who have experienced adverse life effects and have not 'bounced back' can be seen as 'not resilient enough' and their difficulties can be positioned firmly within themselves, as a personal deficit. This overly individualizing narrative can be particularly harmful in the case of children and young people whose needs have traditionally been poorly understood and who are therefore at a particularly high risk of their difficulties being interpreted as a personal deficit rather than a need that requires support.

In the case of autistic girls and women (and, indeed, all autistic people who internalize their difficulties), 'resilience' can become synonymous with their ability to comply and endure what is intolerable for them, for the benefit of those around them. As such, seeing a perceived 'lack of resilience' where the young person is genuinely struggling and unable to cope can deny or delay the implementation of support that they desperately need and may well be legally entitled to. It is also worth being aware of arguments that supposedly prioritize the autistic child's future wellbeing, but ultimately justify the delay or denial of the support they need in that moment in time, such as 'She needs to learn to live in the real world, so she has to *learn* to cope'. While, of course, autistic people should be given support around learning how to navigate a world designed for neurotypical people if they would like that, this is very different to arguing that they should just 'get on with' situations and challenges that they are clearly struggling with.

It is also worth remembering that school isn't strictly 'the real world' either – adults are able, to varying degrees, to make decisions about their lives and careers (i.e., how much social interaction/commuting/time in an office is involved) and about their working, socializing and personal relationship patterns. This freedom rarely exists in the much more rigid context of formal education, where children with very different profiles of strengths and needs have to abide by the same, or very similar, rules and constraints. Therefore, while resilience can be a useful concept in some contexts, we need to ensure that it is not used to promote simplistic narratives about the young person's difficulties that positions them firmly within themselves, with no regard for other, external factors and adaptations that may need to be made.

# CHAPTER 3

# Friendships and Relationships

I have struggled with trusting too much and not wanting to ever give anyone else any reason to dislike me. This can mean overextending myself, not expressing my needs, and not having boundaries (what are boundaries, anyway?!). I have been taken advantage of by people with ill intent and did not immediately recognize what was happening. It is unfathomable to me that people lie and manipulate, as I tend to take others at their word. I end up internalizing deliberate harm by others as a personal failure and inability to discern, which has at times shaken my confidence in myself and in the goodness of the world.

*KD, autistic woman*

Friendship has been a very difficult thing to navigate, and as a result I now have a small friendship circle. Quality over quantity of friends is the way to go (well, for me, at least). I can only manage a low level of socializing and it takes a lot to be trusting of someone (due to past experiences). My friendships would look very different if I wasn't autistic. I also think that my choice of friends would be very different too.

*SB, autistic woman*

Asked to describe an autistic person, many would probably paint the reductive picture of someone who is isolated, has no friends and is altogether uninterested in socializing with others. So crucial is this supposed lack of social skills and withdrawal from social life to our stereotypical image of autism that the very name of the condition is derived from it – the roots of the word lie in the Greek 'autos', meaning 'self', suggesting someone showing no interest in the world outside of themselves. However, having firmly established itself in the popular imagination, this simplistic stereotype may have made it harder to spot autism in the many autistic people who do not conform to it. While some autistic people might fit this profile, there is a lot more subtlety and variability from one autistic person to another. Some may not have an interest in friendships at all, others may desperately want friendships but struggle to initiate those, and there are also many autistic people who seek, have and enjoy friendships. And, when it comes to the 'internalized' or 'masked' presentations of autism, autistic girls' experiences of socializing are often markedly different from those of autistic boys.[27] This pattern is also seen in neurotypical children. It is important to note at this point, however, that as with any research looking at gender differences, this is bound to be reductive and many people will not fall neatly into these supposedly discrete binary categories. Research findings will be presented here, with the caveat that the reality is bound to be much more complicated and nuanced than what can be observed in the context of social and psychological research. All autistic people, regardless of gender, should be treated as individuals first and foremost, but it is useful to have a generic overview of some of the common patterns that tend to emerge.

## Are there any gender-specific differences in social relationships that we can see in autistic girls?

For many years, little was known about autistic girls' friendships and social communication patterns, as most research in this area was carried out with boys.[28] However, this was a major oversight and omission, as we now know that there are some major differences in autistic girls and autistic boys' friendships and socializing patterns. Indeed, some researchers have questioned whether those differences can offer a partial explanation for the delayed – or lack of – diagnosis commonly seen in autistic girls with no learning or language difficulties.[29] Similarly, the very fact that an autistic child has a friend – or a small group of friends – can wrongly be interpreted as a sign that they cannot be autistic if it is (incorrectly) assumed that autistic people do not want or have friends.

Research looking at autistic girls' social skills and relationships, particularly when compared to 1) neurotypical girls, and 2) autistic boys, has found some interesting common themes and key differences. For example, autistic girls' social interaction tends to be more conversation-based, whereas autistic boys' social interaction tends to be more play or activity-based.[30] Additionally, autistic girls are less likely to play on their own compared to autistic boys,[31] which goes against the common stereotype of autistic people as preferring self-led, solitary activities. Again, this could offer a partial explanation as to why some autistic girls' needs go unrecognized for a number of years – the research and, by extension, professionals' knowledge and expectation of how autistic children should – or shouldn't – socialize is based on a profile more commonly seen in boys.

A particularly illuminating study was carried out in the UK by Felicity Sedgewick and colleagues and was published in 2019. Their findings indicated that it is '*gender, rather than diagnosis per se*', that determines the differences in friendships and socializing commonly seen in autistic boys and girls. Specifically, what they found was that while autistic girls have very similar friendship patterns to non-autistic girls, at least on surface level, those tend to be very different to how autistic boys approach social relationships. For example, both neurotypical and autistic girls with no accompanying intellectual difficulties tend to value emotional closeness and support in friendships, whereas boys, regardless of diagnosis, value shared interests and activities. Interestingly, however, there were also some key *qualitative* differences they found in terms of how autistic and non-autistic girls approach and see their friendships. Specifically, they found that:

> autistic girls lacked wider social networks and the friendships they reported were much more intense, with individual best friends often becoming the sole focus of their social lives. Autistic girls also found it much more difficult to understand and manage conflict in their relationships and with their peers generally, and were exposed to more relational bullying (i.e., behaviors such as gossip and being excluded, which are far more predominant in adolescent girls' relationships than any other group).[32]

Additionally, they also found that neurotypical and autistic girls respond differently to those conflicts – while non-autistic girls tend to retaliate in a similar manner, autistic girls 'assume they are entirely to blame for the problem (and do whatever they can to resolve it) or assume that the friendship cannot be rescued (and so withdraw from the relationship)'.[33]

An important aspect of autistic girls' friendship patterns is that they may prefer to have a small group of friends, or one close friend with whom they have a very close and intense relationship.[34] It is possible that this feels more manageable for them compared to having to manage different and chang-ing dynamics in friendships with multiple people; it is also possible that this is because the social aspects of friendships can be difficult to navigate for them, and, as such, they may only have the emotional or social 'battery' for one, rather than multiple close friendships.

However, this raises a couple of important questions – close and intense relationships that involve spending a lot of time together also provide more opportunities for conflict. As we found out previously, managing conflict in friendships can be very difficult for autistic girls and they can withdraw from the friendship. This, in turn, could be highly distressing if they had just one friend – losing the friendship could feel catastrophic in its enormity for the autistic young woman, as she would have lost her main friend, source of support and potentially a neurotypical 'ally' helping her navigate social aspects of school that she would otherwise find challenging. The possible impact of this should not be underestimated and trivialized as typical friendship issues that many young people go through – losing such a major person in her life, even if temporarily, could have a significant negative effect on her mental health, as well as on her ability to attend school, if the friendship was school-based and the friend has moved on and is developing friendships with other people.

In safe, secure relationships, something like telling a friend that I was hurt by something small they said or did feels like an end-of-the-world conflict. I'm in a place in my life and relationships where I'm beginning to do this, even though my nervous system tries its best to make me clam up and run the other way. In therapy, I'm learning to recognize my feelings and wants, which is something I so wish I had been able to do earlier in life.

*KD, autistic woman*

## Stability, control and anxiety: Reflections from practice

There have been a number of instances in my practice where I have heard highly distressed autistic girls be referred to as 'controlling', 'manipulative' and 'dominating' at worst, or 'unkind' and 'needy' at best, for wanting to have one close friend or to maintain proximity to another child – or, in other words, for wanting to have their emotional needs met. Even well-meaning professionals – and adults in general – can resort to simplistic explanations that, intentionally or not, position the 'blame' firmly within the child, with little to no regard to the broader context and the underlying reason for the child's behaviour. For example, if an autistic girl appears to be 'fixated' on one friend and becomes extremely distressed when her friend also wants to explore playing with another child, attributing malicious intent to her reaction is not only simplistic, but it also fails to consider the root cause of the behaviour.

What is often not considered in those cases is that maybe this is the child she feels the safest with or she can only tolerate socializing with one person and having other children join in makes the dynamics too complicated and the conversations too hard to follow. Similarly, a desire to stay in control of a social situation by directing other children's play can be seen as 'domineering', when maintaining a degree of control over the interaction is likely to serve a very specific purpose for some autistic children – keeping the interaction focused on topics that they are familiar with and can comfortably navigate; similarly, this would also ensure a level of predictability and reduce the anxiety usually associated with uncertainty.

Maintaining control is a key tool many autistic people use to manage their anxiety and it should be understood and treated with respect. This does not mean that other children's needs shouldn't be considered and respected, or that the autistic girl shouldn't be supported to explore alternative reactions and ways of approaching the same situation. However, in order to do this effectively, we need to first understand what is causing the underlying anxiety.

We also need to acknowledge the very real power adults hold in shaping narratives around individual children and their needs. Labelling a child as 'manipulative' and 'controlling', rather than exploring the reasons behind their presentation, can easily become an unquestioned, commonly accepted narrative seen as 'the truth' about who they are as a person. Once ingrained, those narratives can be surprisingly resistant to challenge – the adults could then notice or seek out information that seemingly confirms that the child is 'controlling' (a psychological phenomenon known as 'confirmation bias'), which could further consolidate the view that this is who she is in their eyes. Therefore, regardless of the underlying intent, it is important that these narratives are challenged and corrected – behaviour is a form of communication, and labelling the behaviour without trying to understand what it is trying to convey could detract from the child's actual needs – and the support they may need.

## Empathy, girls and autism

As a highly empathetic, creative and imaginative individual, few people outside of the autistic community recognized for a long time that autistics can feel the pain of unselected spoons at the bottom of the drawer, give moving performances on stage, or write convincingly from another's perspective. For a long time when I read about autism, I didn't see myself – only small parts that I related to. There was never enough context to understand how traits could present with great degrees of difference, person to person. It wasn't until I read more accounts online that I came to interpret autistic traits less literally!

*KD, autistic woman*

One of the most pervasive myths about autism is that autistic people are unempathetic.[35] This is sometimes presented as an established, uncontested fact, when the reality is much more nuanced and complicated than that, as we will discover below. Just like anyone else, autistic people can be highly empathetic; however, some social communication and emotion processing differences (i.e., differences around reading emotions and talking about them) can be mistaken for a lack of empathy or emotional detachment. It is worth considering how this narrative can be used to facilitate the 'othering' of autistic people and their portrayal as unemotional and detached as seen in aspects of popular culture, such as in certain films and TV shows.

Even if, for the sake of the argument, we accept that an autistic person is unempathetic, we need to challenge the moral superiority and virtue attributed to empathy – being empathetic doesn't automatically make someone a good, kind or moral person in and of itself, much in the same way as not being conventionally empathetic should not put someone's morality or other personal qualities into question. This assumption becomes particularly problematic when combined with gender stereotypes, where it may be seen as more palatable for a boy or a man to be unempathetic – or to show empathy in an unconventional way – rather than for a girl, as girls and women are stereotypically expected to be caring, kind and selfless in their concern for others. When traditional gender stereotypes are applied, these qualities can be seen as a 'welcome bonus' if observed in men, but an expectation and, indeed, a fundamental characteristic of being female. As such, a girl 'suspected of' being unempathetic, or labelled as unempathetic by others, could potentially be judged more harshly on a social level than a boy.

## Cognitive vs affective empathy

While empathy is often discussed as a single 'ability', it is now believed that it covers several different domains and autistic people may excel in some aspects of those but find others challenging. Therefore, talking about empathy as something a person either does or doesn't have is far too simplistic and bound to be inaccurate. We will consider the two key types, or components of, empathy below.

## COGNITIVE EMPATHY

Cognitive empathy is a person's ability to take on the perspective of another person and imagine or predict how they would think and feel in a given situation.[36] It reflects the 'knowing' aspect of empathy, as opposed to *feeling* what the other person feels. Of course, this capacity for perspective-taking depends in part on one's own experiences – the further away the other person's situation is from our own experiences, the more effortful it would be to imagine and predict their feelings.

It is also important to consider that a person's cognitive empathy may vary depending on the complexity of the situation and whether they have already encountered social scripts for it, either in their own personal experience or indirectly, in books or films, for example. A simple example of this would be being able to imagine or predict how another person would feel if their pet died – a relatively common, albeit sad occurrence, and one that has repeatedly been portrayed in literature and film, thus providing plenty of examples of what that may feel like, even if a person hasn't had a direct experience of it. A slightly more demanding degree of cognitive empathy would be required if, for example, you went to the cinema with several of your friends but forgot to invite one of the girls in the friend group. To empathize with her – to imagine how she would feel and react to being left out – would require actively suppressing your own perspective, such as the knowledge that you did not *consciously choose* to exclude her and that no offence was intended. Some autistic people do indeed struggle with the cognitive aspects of 'putting themselves in someone else's shoes'; however, this does not mean that they are incapable or unwilling to *feel* empathy when they can see that someone is in distress, for example.

What some autistic people struggle with is not so much

feeling or caring for people but building mental models of how people function. In some cases, this difficulty extends to their capacity for self-reflection – for example, as many as 85 per cent of autistic people are believed to experience *alexithymia*, or a difficulty with noticing and interpreting their own emotions and mental states.[37] We can think of self-reflection and cognitive empathy as two sides of the same coin: by observing and interpreting others' actions, children develop insights into human psychology that they can use to enhance their own self-understanding; this introspection in turn allows them to take others' perspectives in situations both real and hypothetical, so the two processes should be mutually reinforcing. Conversely, a difficulty with one of these is likely to also result in difficulties in the other.

It should be clear then that what appears to external observers as a lack of care and interest in others in *some* autistic people could actually be born out of a general difficulty with *building mental models of other people's thoughts and feelings*, rather than due to lack of care or interest in other people. This distinction, however, is rarely drawn when autism and empathy is discussed, and autistic people's supposed lack of concern for other people's feelings is presented as fact – despite the far more complicated reality, and plenty of examples of the opposite.

## AFFECTIVE/EMOTIONAL EMPATHY

Affective or emotional empathy refers to the ability to *feel* other people's feelings as our own, such as the feeling of deep sadness when watching reports of a war or the aftermath of a natural disaster on the news.[38] In that sense, affective empathy is perhaps closer to what most people seem to mean when they talk about empathy – the ability to feel others' pain and joy, rather than the ability to construct mental models with predictive power, which is what some autistic people struggle with.

Research has indicated that autistic people show similar levels of affective empathy to non-autistic people,[39] and yet, the myth about autistic people's supposed lack of empathy has remained popular. Indeed, this myth is the one I come across most often in my practice and it seems to be applied to many different expressions of autism, from non-speaking autistic children with accompanying learning difficulties to highly articulate autistic teenagers. On occasions, I have seen professionals question the diagnosis of a child or a young person on the basis of the fact that they can, in fact, be empathetic – 'But she is very kind to the other children/animals/her family'; 'She gets very upset when another child has hurt themselves and can't stop thinking about it and asking questions, i.e., whether they're okay.' This shows how this myth is perceived, at least by some, as 'common knowledge' and as a fundamental, defining trait of autism.

## Hyper-empathy

Some autistic people are not only highly empathetic, but they experience overwhelming, even debilitating, empathy for other people, animals or even fictional characters, to an extent where they can become overwhelmed due to the sheer intensity of the feeling. It is important to consider how this may also be linked to the strong sense of justice and fairness many autistic people have – it is possible that some autistic people's highly empathetic responses could be related to the fact that it is fundamentally unfair when another person suffers as a result of war/illness/discrimination/poverty/homelessness or when a stray animal is hungry or in pain, for example. Unfortunately, there is little to no research specifically exploring hyper-empathy in autistic people. The majority of what we know is based on the accounts actually autistic people have generously shared or through anecdotal practice observations. It is an unfortunate fact about the state of the literature at present that it is overwhelmingly focused on autistic people's perceived 'deficits', with less of a focus on areas that challenge or add nuance to some of those long-held beliefs and stereotypes. This is slowly changing, with many more researchers recognizing the need to consult with and, indeed, include autistic people and fellow autistic researchers in those explorations. However, some concepts and aspects of autism such as hyper-empathy remain under-researched.

## Romantic relationships and friendships in adolescence and adulthood

Autistic women's experiences of romantic relationships and friendships in adolescence and adulthood is another area that has not been researched as thoroughly as it deserves. Despite this, some of the studies that have taken place have provided interesting and useful insights into how autistic young women manage their personal relationships and the challenges they may face. It is important to first consider how the myth that autistic people are unempathetic or somewhat unconcerned with other people's opinions or with social interactions may play a particularly significant role here. Specifically, if we accept those ideas at face value without getting to know the individual person, we may fail to spot that autistic young women can, in fact, be very eager to please those around them and to fit in, even when this is to the detriment of their own happiness, comfort, interests or safety. We also need to consider how difficulties with making sense of social situations could result in difficulties and vulnerabilities in personal relationships in adulthood. While we shouldn't assume that all autistic young women are vulnerable purely on the basis of being autistic – this would be far too reductionist and simplistic – we do need to be aware of some of the potential challenges they may face.

Felicity Sedgewick and colleagues carried out a study with autistic and neurotypical women between the ages of 20 and 40 to find out how autistic women's relationships and friendships may differ from those of non-autistic women.[40] While they found many similarities, as is also the case during childhood and early adolescence, they also found that autistic women:

> found it harder to interpret social situations, and generally reported having more difficult friendship/relationship experiences than neurotypical women. This was especially true in terms of social and sexual experiences, where autistic women reported that they were much more vulnerable to exploitation than neurotypical women. Autistic women themselves linked this to their difficulties interpreting social situations. Despite these difficulties though, autistic women were happier with their relationships and much more confident in their social skills in adulthood than they remembered being as teenagers.[41]

One crucial factor we need to bear in mind when thinking about relationships and autistic girls is safeguarding. While risk of exploitation isn't necessarily restricted to a specific time period, the teenage years are a time when young people, both autistic and neurotypical, try to figure out their place in the world, form new relationships and learn to establish boundaries. In the case of autistic girls and young women, it is important to consider how the combination of 1) struggling to read social cues or detect hidden agendas, 2) being eager to fit in and please others and 3) being a young woman learning to navigate the world could increase their risk of being targeted for exploitation. Safeguarding should, therefore, be at the forefront of the thinking of professionals – and all adults – supporting autistic young women. That is not to say that negative assumptions should be made about autistic young women and their capacity to make decisions about their lives; rather, it is important to acknowledge that autistic people, regardless of gender, can be targeted for exploitation, and girls and women may face a unique set of challenges and vulnerabilities.

---

Friendships and relationships are definitely heavily impacted by being autistic. I think, unfortunately, I have come to now recognize that I am vulnerable in ways others might be less likely to be. I tend to see the best in everyone and have definitely been taken advantage of in the past, as well as being gaslit often because I take communication on board differently and have previous trauma. Society has taught me that I am in the wrong and that the way I experience the world isn't real – and that bleeds into how I experience my relationships. I have also often lost friends because of my tone of voice or because I have been rude, but in ways I do not realize I am being.

*Charli Clement, autistic non-binary person*

We are vulnerable to predators. We can find ourselves in dangerous situations without the least idea of how to get out.

*KD, autistic woman*

Another small-scale study identified interesting themes that emerged for adult autistic women in terms of their intimate relationships.[42] It is important to bear in mind, though, that the study had a small sample size (number of participants) and, as such, the themes reported may be more reflective of the individual participants' views, rather than a more general pattern – so they need to be interpreted and generalized with caution. Nevertheless, they provide some interesting common themes. Specifically, some of the autistic women who took part in the research reported:

- having difficulty with understanding their partners (expressing care in different ways; finding it hard to remember that others might not read a situation in the same way as them or have the same interests; maintaining focus on their partner to meet their emotional needs and filtering out distractions)

- having difficulty with managing the spontaneous nature of a relationship (need for clear rules and routines, not just in daily life but in all romantic relationships; the need for moments of solitude)

- concerns about the future of relationships (being able to cope with the changing demands and dynamics of the relationship; concerns about not being able to hide her difficulties as the relationship becomes more intimate; anxiety around the prospect of having children together).

The authors did, however, also identify that autistic women valued several aspects of romantic relationships, such as the opportunity to explore activities and joint interests together, and the reciprocity and companionship that intimate relation-ships bring, alongside the rewarding feeling of having formed a close connection to another person.

# CHAPTER 4

# Puberty, Menstruation and Personal Care

I was unable to understand the expectations of me, particularly in puberty. I wasn't educated about my developing body by either my parents or the education system. I was terrified when my period started, totally shocked by the blood and at a loss as to what to do. I was aware of periods as I had been bullied by the girls in my class as I was late, the last girl in the class, to start mine. So, I was desperate for my periods to start and ill-prepared for what they actually were or how I would feel when they started. I had no one I could go to with any questions about it.

I remember my mum being surprised when I developed bodily hair, embarrassing me in front of a group of people by stating that I was starting to get 'hairy armpits'. No discussion of what I should do about this was open to me. I really wish that the adults around me had understood the importance of educating me in my developing body, how to take care of myself and the importance of consent. Whilst I understand that this was strongly influenced by the era in which I grew up in and my parents being uncomfortable to be open about such topics, it really is critical that adults of autistic girls and boys provide them with safe and open information in order for them to keep themselves safe and well.

Hormones had a *big* impact on me in puberty. My mum loves to tell everyone how I went from being a quiet, sweet-natured girl to some kind of shouting and outspoken monster overnight!

I now understand that I was having meltdowns at home on a regular basis, which I was shamed for and I was often scared that I had little or no control over these explosive outbursts. There was a liberation in being a teenager and experimenting with my image and starting to understand the thrill of being outspoken and sarcastic!

*AA, autistic woman*

Puberty, with the associated physical, emotional and identity changes, has long been known to be a tumultuous period for young people, regardless of whether they are neurodivergent or not. Talking with young people about those changes and the challenges they pose can be uncomfortable for adults who may then avoid conversations that might turn 'awkward', or only briefly touch upon certain topics that they are more comfortable discussing. While coming to terms with the various changes that take place during puberty can be challenging for all young people, it is likely to be particularly difficult for autistic young people, who often have a strong preference for routine and can find changes – especially ones they have no control over – exceptionally anxiety-provoking and hard to process.

It is also important to consider the profound nature of some of the changes that take place during puberty – not only are they completely outside the control of the young person, but they affect and change fundamental aspects of themselves, such as their bodies and emotions. For young people who already experience sensory processing needs, seeing – and feeling – your body change, when you have no control over that, may be profoundly unnerving and distressing. Similarly, when making sense of emotions is already difficult, experiencing mood changes and reacting more intensively in certain situations as a result of hormonal changes is likely to be confusing and unsettling. Teenagers' experiences are not always discussed with the respect they deserve, and flippant and dismissive comments that trivialize young people's distress (e.g., 'You're not really depressed, that's just being a teenager'; 'Stop talking back, it must be the hormones talking') fail to acknowledge the very real impact the changes that take place during puberty can have on their wellbeing.

---

I think puberty was mainly challenging due to the hormones and emotions that were changed during that time, and it felt like it was such an unstable time with a lot of outside pressure, particularly from education and trying to set up what the rest of your life would look like. I think what I want adults to know about puberty: it's just remembering how difficult it is to go through that period of time, getting older and being able to reflect back is completely different to being in the midst of it.

*SO, autistic woman*

---

Additionally, to make matters even more complicated, issues surrounding women's bodies and health – such as menstruation, for example – can also be perceived as something private that should not be discussed openly. Navigating the minefield of adolescence as an autistic young woman can be overwhelming and it is perhaps unsurprising that autistic women's difficulties often escalate during the teenage years. Having frank and open discussions, both at home and at school, is particularly important in helping alleviate some of that pressure. However, as a first step, we need to understand which aspects of puberty and adolescence are likely to be particularly challenging for autistic young women.

## Changing bodies

The body changes that take place during puberty in young women – such as weight gain, widened hips, development of breasts, body hair growth, acne, increased sweating – can pose a range of challenges for autistic girls. While puberty and the body changes that take place during this period affect all autistic people to varying degrees, we need to be mindful of some of the unique challenges autistic girls and women are likely to face and how those may be further exacerbated by societal expectations around women's bodies.

For example, while the reductionist stereotype of teenage boys' personal hygiene supposedly leaving a lot to be desired is often treated as something normal and to be expected, this light-hearted, magnanimous attitude is rarely extended to girls. Girls are often expected to be 'classy' and 'ladylike', which usually entails a set of very specific expectations in terms of the way they look, dress and behave (e.g., clean, tidy and 'put together'; talking about periods or bodily functions is 'private' and best avoided as a conversation topic). The onset of puberty can, therefore, mark the beginning of a range of expectations and routines that are profoundly uncomfortable for some autistic young women on a sensory level. For example, wearing a bra can be experienced as not just uncomfortable, but intolerable; however, the societal expectation that talking about such matters is not appropriate, combined with the desire to fit in and not draw attention to oneself, may result in autistic girls accepting the distress and discomfort they experience as unavoidable.

Similarly, the growth of body hair can cause sensory processing challenges of its own – some autistic young women may be very sensitive to body hair touching or brushing against clothes, whereas others may find the experience of hair removal profoundly distressing on a sensory level, while feeling pressure to do so regardless, due to the societal expectation for women to have hair-free bodies. While some progress has arguably been made in recent years in terms of challenging those expectations, social norms are notoriously slow to shift and, during the period of development when 'fitting in' is seen as socially important, autistic girls may feel pressured to conform to those established stereotypes, even when this causes them sensory distress.

## Personal care

While parents and carers can have a more active role in managing aspects of personal care for children when they are of primary school age, and the difficulties of autistic girls may not be immediately obvious at that point, those may become more noticeable and pronounced with age. While this trend applies to all autistic people regardless of gender, we need to consider some of the unique challenges likely to be faced by girls.

## Haircuts

Getting a haircut, when broken down into the individual steps involved in the process, can be an overwhelming process for autistic people due to the sensory, tactile (touch-related) and social demands of being in a hair salon. The importance placed on young women's appearance could make hair maintenance and trips to the hairdresser seem 'unavoidable' or 'essential' for them, which wouldn't necessarily be the case for young men. A trip to the hairdresser, however, involves several key components that could be challenging for an autistic person to navigate – social interaction when booking an appointment, as well as 'small talk' with the hairdresser. Similarly, on a sensory level, having one's hair cut may involve, amongst others, a stranger touching your head, scalp and hair, pulling your hair while brushing it, washing the hair, with the associated feeling of cold, wet strands of hair touching the face, as well as the noise of hairdryers, harsh, fluorescent lighting in salons and noise from other people's conversations. Hair maintenance appointments are often presented as 'pampering' or 'self-care' rituals that should be enjoyable and desirable for women, and while this may be the case for some, it is important that we consider the very real challenges autistic young women may face in this context.

## Showering

For neurotypical people with no sensory processing needs, taking a shower or a bath may be a calming and refreshing experience that soothes them after a long day or prepares them for the day ahead. However, this may be a very different experience for an autistic person; showers can be noisy, and the feeling of water being projected onto the skin at speed, the sensation of wet hair on the skin and water entering the eyes and ears can be an exceptionally difficult combination of sensory input to tolerate. Similarly, while taking a bath can be a pleasant experience for some autistic people, for others, being wet, the changes in water temperature and changes to skin texture can be a sensory challenge.

It is also worth remembering that showers and baths involve multiple steps and transitions, which can be a challenge for autistic people with executive functioning difficulties – or difficulties with planning, organization and task initiation. For example, planning which products to take into the shower or bath, or the multiple steps involved in washing both one's body and hair, including the use of different products depending on hair type. Additionally, taking a bath and showering also require a transition from the bathroom back to the room, which can feel colder and pose sensory challenges around drying skin and hair, putting on clothes that may feel different against freshly washed skin, as well as draining the bath, and remembering to put any products used back in their place.

### Brushing hair

Hair brushing is another personal care routine that can be deeply unpleasant and painful on a sensory level, particularly for autistic people with longer hair. As with other aspects of personal care, it is important to consider how girls who struggle with hair brushing in the morning may be perceived and judged socially, compared to boys, where the expectation to look 'put together' is less strong and socially ingrained.

## Brushing teeth

Teeth brushing involves its own set of sensory challenges, such as the sensation of cold water and the toothbrush against one's teeth and gums; the taste – and aftertaste – of the toothpaste, which can be a profoundly uncomfortable experience that some autistic children and young people may, understandably, be keen to avoid.

## Getting dressed and clothing

Getting dressed in the morning and deciding what clothes to wear is a surprisingly complex process – a child or a young person needs to be able to plan ahead and judge what type of clothing will be appropriate for the weather, consider what type of clothing would be appropriate for the occasion and have the fine and gross motor skills required to physically get dressed. Clothes can also vary considerably in terms of fabric, fit, how they feel against the skin, how absorbent they are and how comfortable they are to wear over the course of the day. School uniforms and shoes can be particularly uncomfortable due to the fabric and fit, as well as the lack of flexibility that often surrounds school uniform rules. This could mean that, before the school day has even started, an autistic child or young person's stress levels are already heightened, and they have to attempt to stay focused and engage with learning while also experiencing sensory overload.

## Personal care and girls: High expectations

The sensory challenges above are certainly not unique to girls, and many autistic people, regardless of gender, experience those. However, a key point to consider is whether girls may face higher expectations when it comes to their appearance and grooming routines, and how this may be perceived by those around them. For example, a girl who avoids taking showers or brushing her hair or teeth due to the sensory overload may be judged more harshly on a social level compared to a boy, as the (very simplistic, stereotypical) idea that boys are often keen to avoid personal care routines and need reminders is more normalized and accepted socially under the reductionist guise of 'boys will be boys'.

## Menstruation

I started my periods quite early compared to most of my peers at the time, at age 11. I knew about them beforehand as I'd discussed it with my mum and read books very young but struggled with the reality. I wish people understood that puberty is difficult for all young people, but this is extremely amplified for autistic individuals who struggle with any change alongside new sensory experiences.

This is partly because sensory experiences are both external and internal in the case of periods. There is the sensory overwhelm from the period itself, including pain, nausea and dealing with changing period products. For many of us, the period also exacerbates existing sensory needs and leads to meltdowns and shutdowns becoming more common or difficult. This is particularly hard to process because your body, emotions and needs are different every single week as you go through ovulation, the period and stages in between. It can be so hard to process the changes as they are often unpredictable and constantly different; there is almost no way to get used to them.

At the time, alternative period products like period pants

weren't very common, but for young people with periods now, I'd highly recommend that adults around them support finding the most comfortable products for them. I think it is also crucial to understand how their cycle might be exacerbating their other autistic traits, and the fact that some studies show we may experience periods more heavily or more painfully and are more likely to experience PMDD [premenstrual dysphoric disorder] – we aren't exaggerating.

*Charli Clement, autistic non-binary person*

Menstruation and the sensory challenges it brings is rarely discussed in the context of autistic girls' needs – indeed, there are only a handful of academic papers exploring this essential question. It is also important to contextualize this lack of research and understanding within the broader context of women's health, some aspects of which have historically been seen as a taboo and something that should not be discussed publicly.

For an autistic girl who has sensory processing differences, the onset of menstruation may feel like a sensory assault on several levels that lasts several days and she has no control over, including bloating and stomach cramps, the sensation of leaking blood on a sanitary pad, inserting a tampon, dealing with leaks and stains while at school, the smell of blood and having to judge when a sanitary product needs to be changed. Additionally, menstruation can also have an impact on emotions and one's mood, which can be particularly distressing for autistic young people who may already struggle with making sense of their emotions. To complicate matters further, periods are never exactly the same, and the sometimes-unpredictable nature of the 'side effects' associated with them make having a clear routine around them very difficult.

Similarly, premenstrual syndrome (PMS) symptoms can also be unpredictable and distressing on a sensory and emotional level, as those can include anything from headaches and mood changes to tenderness in the body and even gum pain. This lack of control and predictability can lead to an increase in anxiety and worry about the period coinciding with an important exam, PE or a school trip, for example. Similarly, this uncertainty can be further exacerbated as the length of the menstrual cycle can vary and periods may be irregular to begin with, making it harder to plan and prepare for them. The stigma surrounding periods can also mean that autistic girls 'suffer in silence' and are unable to openly discuss how their periods affect them and access appropriate support.

Another important aspect of menstruation is the level of planning required in terms of ensuring that sanitary products are at hand at the right time (which can be hard to predict for those with irregular periods). As many autistic people struggle with executive functioning, including planning and organization, these tasks can be very challenging to manage and plan effectively, which could lead to anxiety.

In an article called '"Life is much more difficult to manage during periods": Autistic experiences of menstruation', authors Robyn Steward and colleagues outlined the findings of one of the very few studies looking at autistic girls' experiences of periods.[43] Their findings were concerning, albeit unsurprising – they concluded that, for autistic women who took part in the research, periods were 'particularly difficult and distressing', with increased difficulties with sensory processing and emotional and executive regulation. They reported 'overwhelmingly negative experiences' linked to menstruation, with negative implications for women's ability to engage in daily social and employment-related activities.

# CHAPTER 5

# Mental Health

Being women means we have a higher pressure to mask (and sadly a need too). [...] alongside our autism, we may also be masking our mental health difficulties. Sometimes we can look okay, when we are in fact not. Sometimes it may take the right person (who we trust) to ask the right questions to find out we are struggling a lot more than we are letting on.

*SB, autistic woman*

It isn't inevitable, but we're made to feel as if poor mental health or distress is an inevitability for us.

*SO, autistic woman*

- Autistic women are *13 times more likely to die by suicide* than non-autistic women and two times more likely to die by suicide than autistic men.[44]

- *32% of autistic women* under the age of 25 are *hospitalized for a mental health condition*, compared to 5% of non-autistic women.[45]

- '[...] autism is associated with an *83% increased risk of self-harm* among females and a 47% increased risk among males'.[46]

- Autistic pupils are *47 times more likely to experience school distress* compared to non-autistic pupils.[47]

An autistic person doesn't become autistic on the day of their diagnosis – they have been autistic all their life and are likely to have missed out on support up until that point. This does also mean that, if they were struggling prior to their diagnosis, their difficulties may have been misdiagnosed. While autism can and does co-occur with a range of mental health conditions, as we will see below, the issues of misdiagnosis or diagnostic over-shadowing are particularly important in the context of late-di-agnosed autistic people, such as autistic girls. We will explore these important issues and the impact of a lack of diagnosis or misdiagnosis on autistic girls' wellbeing and access to support.

An entire book can be written on the topic of autism and mental health, but this chapter is not intended as an exhaus-tive, academic summary of what is a very big field – that would be an impossible task. Instead, we will consider some of the key areas, conditions and issues within the broad field of mental health that are of relevance to autistic girls and women, based on the literature and my own practice. For a more in-depth exploration of each of these areas, see the Recommended Reading and Resources at the end of the book.

## What is 'alexithymia' and how is it relevant to autistic people's mental health?

First, we need to familiarize ourselves with key terms that will contextualize and help explain some of the difficulties autistic people are more likely to face. One such concept is 'alexithymia' (pronounced ah-lexi-thai-meah) – an inability, or difficulty with, processing and recognizing emotions, as well as a focus on external, concrete experiences or information, rather than internal ones.[48] It is important to emphasize that this is not about an *intellectual* or *linguistic* understanding of emotion words – some autistic people may well be able to give an accurate, dictionary-style, factual definition of the word; rather, alexithymia refers to the processing and ability to monitor and recognize emotional states. Alexithymia is very common amongst autistic people – a 2019 meta-analysis (an exploration of all the available literature on a given topic) indicated that alexithymia is *10 times as prevalent* in autistic people compared to non-autistic people, with a prevalence of just under 50 per cent and just under 5 per cent in autistic and non-autistic people respectively.[49] While not all autistic people will also experience alexithymia, with prevalence rates so high, it is of fundamental importance that the possibility is always considered and investigated.

This is important for several reasons – first, if an autistic person is unable to identify their emotions, they may struggle to notice triggers in their environment that could overwhelm them, and make links between emotions, thoughts and behaviour. This is particularly relevant if an autistic child is asked to 'reflect' on their behaviour at school following an incident, for example, or in cases where well-meaning professionals and adults in general ask them to 'tell us what you think will be helpful/what your triggers are'. While the intention behind this may be very good and the adult's aim may be to make sure that the young person's voice is heard, which is critically important, we need to consider that some autistic people will find identifying triggers and how those link to their emotions exceptionally challenging. A more structured, guided approach would be more suitable instead, where the young person is provided with 'scaffolding' to help articulate their thoughts, e.g., 'I noticed that you seemed to look confused and worried when the teacher asked you to go into groups – I wonder whether you felt anxious at that moment, because you were worried about having to speak to the other students?'

It is also important to bear in mind that some therapeutic approaches, such as Cognitive Behavioural Therapy, rely heavily on the individual's ability to reflect on their own thoughts and feelings, and how those link to behaviours. While some people, including some autistic people, may respond well to this approach, others who have difficulty identifying and monitoring their own emotions are likely to struggle more. This highlights the need for careful assessment and an individual approach when it comes to therapeutic work with autistic people, as one size really does not fit all, and practitioners need to be prepared to make adaptations and consider carefully which approach would be most suitable.

---

Repeated illness, burnout and autistic burnout, which is often mistaken for depression, are all signs of our autism that must be discussed and explored in depth, to prevent more serious mental or physical illness down the line.

[...] successful jobs, long-term relationships and children do not indicate that there is not a struggle. Our ability to 'mask' our bewilderment and exhaustion needs a non-judgemental and curious professional who genuinely understands the risk of dismissing a courageous woman who is sharing her concerns and often well-researched questions.

I wish the medical and psychology profession would take

more seriously the need to research how autism presents in girls and women, to see more widely the patterns of misdiagnosis which at its most serious consequence can reduce the lifespan of unidentified autistic girls and women.

*AA, autistic woman*

## Autistic burnout

Another important term we need to be aware of is 'autistic burnout' – a concept often used within the autistic community but severely under-researched and largely missing from the academic literature up until as recently as 2020.[50] Autistic burnout refers to a state of deep exhaustion, withdrawal, inability to perform daily tasks and overall loss of functioning that is distinct from depression but could lead to suicidal thoughts. It is considered to be a response to having to camouflage or mask one's autism in a neurotypical world, which can be exceptionally laborious and can have a profoundly negative impact on autistic people's mental health. Considering that the literature is still in its infancy and only a handful of research articles have been published to date, there isn't yet a commonly agreed definition of autistic burnout. However, several studies in the past three years have tried to define it based on interviews with autistic people and the common themes that emerged from their responses.

In one of the first papers published on this topic in 2020, Dora Raymaker and colleagues found that autistic burnout is:

characterized by pervasive, long-term (typically 3+ months) exhaustion, loss of function, and reduced tolerance to stimulus.[51]

What they meant by 'reduced tolerance to stimulus' was anything from sensory overload, such as loud noises, to attendance of social events. The study also suggested that autistic burnout is distinct from depression and other types of burnout (such as work-based burnout, where the term originated from), and specific to autistic people. Additionally, they found that autistic burnout negatively affected autistic people's quality of life and the participants spoke about 'a lack of empathy from neurotypical people'. We will come back to this point later on in the chapter, when we discuss school distress and emotionally-based school non-attendance, where it is particularly relevant.

Another study carried out by Julianne Higgins and colleagues in 2021 defined autistic burnout as a:

> highly debilitating condition characterised by exhaustion, withdrawal, executive function problems and generally reduced functioning, with increased manifestation of autistic traits – and distinct from depression and non-autistic burnout.[52]

Similarly, a 2023 study by Samuel Arnold and colleagues identified:

> a core phenomenon, comprising exhaustion, withdrawal and cognitive overload, associated with stressors potentially unique to autistic people.[53]

We can see that, based on all these definitions, *extreme exhaustion* and *withdrawal* are key characteristics of autistic burnout, alongside more general difficulties with reduced functioning and inability to maintain camouflaging and masking of autistic traits. It is of fundamental importance that clinicians, education professionals and, indeed, anyone who works with autistic people are familiar with the concept of autistic burn-out – failure to recognize it could result in lack of recognition, or misdiagnosis, of the autistic person's needs. For example, while autistic burnout may appear very similar to depression at first glance, failure to recognize the underlying origin of the autistic person's distress (e.g., overload from constant masking and camouflaging) could result in 1) leaving the underlying stressors unidentified and unaddressed and 2) therapeutic approaches that are not suitably adapted for autistic people which, in turn, could lead to further withdrawal and increase the need for masking. This could further exacerbate the exhaustion and burnout, and can ultimately become a self-perpetuating cycle of masking, exhaustion and distress.

## Autistic burnout in girls and women

Autistic burnout appears to occur at least partially as a result of the long-term negative effect of masking and camouflaging autistic traits in a world that is designed to fit the needs of neurotypical people. We do, therefore, need to consider what this means for a group of autistic people that is particularly likely to mask and camouflage – autistic girls and women – as they may be at a higher risk of autistic burnout. Researcher Jane Mantzalas and colleagues raise another important point in a paper discussing factors that increase or decrease the risk of autistic burnout:

> Unique factors associated with being female such as menstrua-tion, menopause (Moseley et al., 2020; Steward et al., 2018), and pregnancy and childbirth (Samuel et al., 2021) may contribute to a greater risk of autistic burnout among females as these experiences are often associated with heightened sensory

difficulties and anxiety, poorer executive functioning, and a reduced capacity for emotion regulation.[54]

While the research on autistic burnout is still in its infancy and our understanding of autistic women's experiences of autistic burnout is far from where it should be, we know enough to recognize that this is a serious issue that is likely to affect many autistic women's quality of life, as well as their ability to function socially, emotionally, and in an educational and workplace environment.

## Autistic meltdowns

Autistic meltdowns are involuntary and unintentional intense reactions or responses to situations or environments that are overwhelming for the autistic person. It is important to emphasize that autistic meltdowns are usually outside of the control of the individual and tend to be a sign that they have reached a 'breaking point', where they can no longer mask. When this happens, the autistic person may act in a way that is uncharacteristic for them (e.g., shouting, swearing, throwing or breaking objects, crying) and they may be very exhausted and/or embarrassed after a meltdown, especially if it happened in a public space. There are many different potential meltdown triggers and those will vary from one individual to another; however, examples could include being overwhelmed by the noise in the classroom, feeling criticized or put 'on the spot', or an unexpected change – however 'minor' this may seem to those around them.

It is important to recognize that autistic meltdowns are not 'tantrums', 'attention seeking' or 'aggressive behaviour' – even if the autistic person is communicating their distress in a way that may seem anger-driven. Rather, they are an expression of the level of distress they are in, and the subsequent loss of control is unintentional, rather than a deliberately defiant behaviour. Additionally, in light of the fact that alexithymia is very common in autistic people, emotional regulation and identifying triggers in advance is likely to be a challenge for some autistic people and could potentially make them more prone to becoming overwhelmed.

Another key point to consider is how intense emotional reactions during autistic meltdowns can be interpreted – or misinterpreted – in girls and women. Specifically, autistic girls' distress can be interpreted as a sign of 'emotional instability' or being 'hysterical' – which would fall conveniently in line with some long-established gender stereotypes. This has the potential to cause a lot of harm both in the immediate and long term, by ignoring the root cause of their distress and labelling their distress as a primarily behavioural or mental health need. This could result in both lack of suitable support and potential misdiagnosis. For example, an autistic woman whose autism hasn't been recognized might initially be diagnosed with another condition, such as emotionally unstable personality disorder or bipolar disorder, for example; while autism can and does co-occur with some mental health conditions and these are not necessarily mutually exclusive, the potential for misdiagnosis is also high, considering the gender bias in autism diagnosis. We will consider this in more detail in the 'Misdiagnosis and diagnostic overshadowing' section of this chapter.

## Autistic shutdowns
An autistic shutdown can happen for very similar reasons

as an autistic meltdown – feeling overwhelmed, anxious and reaching a tipping point beyond which the anxiety can no longer be contained. A shutdown, however, can be far less obvious and harder to spot – for example, during a shutdown, the child might withdraw, stop talking or responding completely, and may go to a quiet, empty space to self-regulate (e.g., a resource cupboard at school or in their room or bed at home). A shutdown might not be spotted immediately in an autistic girl, especially if she is seen as 'quiet and shy'. This could result in an accumulation of anxiety over time and, if the reasons for her shutdowns remain unaddressed, she may no longer be able to tolerate being at school (or any other environment that is proving overwhelming).

## Mental health conditions and autistic girls and women: What are the generic trends?

We are extremely at risk of anxiety, depression, burnout, suicidal ideation and suicidal completion. We experience barriers accessing supports and being believed about our suffering. All autistics need support, whether or not it looks like we have it all together. As our needs vary individual to individual, day to day and situation to situation, we need access to an individualized approach to resources and services.

*KD, autistic woman*

Autistic girls and women are at an exponential risk of developing mental health difficulties compared to non-autistic people and even autistic boys and men. One recent study illustrates this alarming trend clearly. Miriam Martini and colleagues collected and analysed a huge amount of data on more than 1,330,000 people born in Sweden between 2001 and 2013.[55] They found the following (illustrated in Figure 4.1):

- Autistic women are more likely than autistic men and non-autistic people to have any type of psychiatric diagnosis, especially anxiety, depression and sleep disorders.

- 14.7% of autistic men had an anxiety disorder diagnosis, but for autistic women the rate was more than double that – 31.9%. This means that approximately 1 in every 3 young women in Sweden with an autism diagnosis is also diagnosed with anxiety. For non-autistic men and women, the rates were much lower – only 2.5% of men and 5.4% of women had the diagnosis.

- A similar ratio was found for depression: 18.4% of autistic men versus 31% of autistic women (compared with just 2.6% and 5.2% of non-autistic men and women, respectively).

It is important to emphasize that this data only includes cases of *diagnosed* autism and *diagnosed* mental health problems, so the actual rates of these problems among un- or misdiagnosed autistic women are likely to be much higher. Anecdotally, in my experience of working with autistic young people, the rates of anxiety and sleep differences in particular are considerably higher than the already alarmingly high rates reported in the study. These may not always be detected but, if they are, they may be seen as going 'hand-in-hand' with autism, so seeking a further diagnosis may be seen as unnecessary.

Autistic people in general, regardless of gender, are at a higher risk of being diagnosed with a mental health condition. However, as we can see from the data in Figure 4.2, autistic women are consistently at a higher risk of developing a range of mental health conditions compared to both non-autistic people and autistic men.

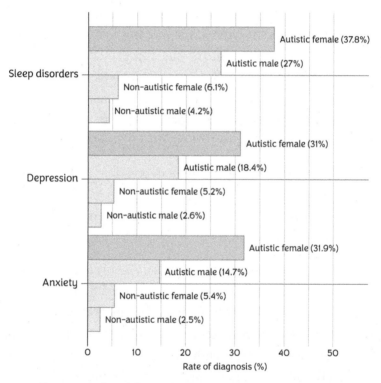

*Figure 4.1: Rates of diagnosis of sleep disorders, depression and anxiety amongst autistic and non-autistic women and men*
Adapted from Martini *et al.* (2022)

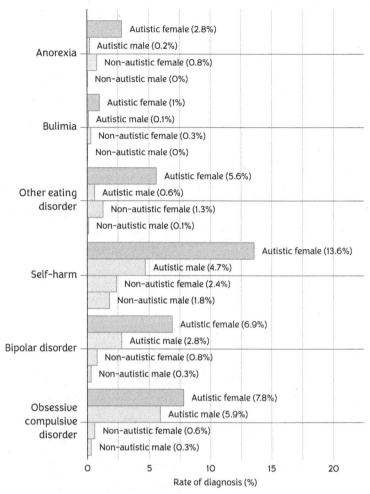

*Figure 4.2: Rates of diagnosis for eating disorders, self-harm, bipolar disorder and obsessive compulsive disorder amongst autistic and non-autistic women and men*
Adapted from Martini *et al.* (2022)

Again, we need to bear in mind that these findings reflect trends only in people who have been diagnosed with both autism *and* a mental health condition – considering the barriers to diagnosis faced by autistic girls and women we discussed in Chapter 1, the rates may be even higher. Another important point to consider is that the study findings are based on a Swedish sample, so they may not necessarily be generalizable to other countries as there may be regional variations in terms of how diagnoses are given and recorded. Nevertheless, other studies, albeit with much smaller sample sizes (number of participants who took part), highlight very similar trends. For example, a study with participants from Australia identified the rates of depression and anxiety are very high amongst autistic people, with autistic women being at a particularly high risk of both anxiety and depression.[56] Specifically, 50 per cent of autistic women and 30 per cent of autistic men in the sample had anxiety, and 55.8 per cent of autistic women and 26.5 per cent of autistic men had depression.

## Depression

While we have established that autistic women are at a higher risk of depression, we need to consider how this may interact with the 'internalizing' presentation of autism. Depression itself is sometimes viewed as an internalized presentation of psychological distress, so there is inevitably going to be some overlap between depression and the experience of having to mask and repress the anxiety and overwhelm caused by being autistic in a neurotypical world. As we have seen, because autism is more likely to go unnoticed and unrecognized in people with the 'internalizing' presentation, their needs will often not be met consistently, which may result in autistic burnout. It is important to emphasize that this burnout is the predictable outcome of being forced to tolerate exceptional levels of stress for months and years on end, without reprieve.

Although the limited research literature on the topic views autistic burnout as distinct from depression in its origins and nature,[57] the two may often present as almost indistinguishable in practice. This confusion can lead some to *individualize* the autistic person's difficulties, misinterpreting them as 'within-person' problems, rather than as the result of being overwhelmed and not having their needs met. In cases where the autistic person's distress is rooted in burnout and overwhelm, rather than depression on its own, attempting to provide psychological support without addressing the underlying causes may not be as productive if the autistic person then has to return and endure the same conditions that led to burnout in the first place. Instead, the problem must be properly identified and addressed on multiple levels, including with environmental adaptations.

We also need to consider that, as we have already seen earlier on in the chapter, autistic women are at a disproportionate risk of both suicide and self-harm:

> autistic females had an 83% increased risk and autistic males had a 47% increased risk of self-harm compared with nonautistic individuals, when accounting for neighborhood income and rurality, intellectual disabilities, and psychiatric diagnoses.[58]

For many of us, suicide or self-harm will thankfully be something that we have not been affected by directly. This does, however, mean that the prospect of someone hurting themselves or taking their own life due to the level of distress they are in can seem like a distant, unlikely and hypothetical possibility – something that happens to other people, not to someone we know. Unfortunately, research tells us that this is a very real risk for many autistic girls and women, who, staggeringly, are 13 times more likely to die by suicide than non-autistic women. This shows how incredibly high the stakes are – we cannot be complacent and passive observers of autistic girls' distress. In the case of services or institutions working with autistic young women, failing to recognize their needs and put in place the support they need, when they need it, can have disastrous consequences – even if those were never intended. A proactive rather than a reactive approach is, therefore, essential.

## Anxiety

I received treatment for anxiety and depression and was told that my anxiety was often related to social situations. [...] I later realized that this wasn't just anxiety or depression, rather the manifestations of an autistic distress.

*SO, autistic woman*

As with depression, the rates of anxiety in autistic people, and autistic women in particular, are disproportionately high – in fact, they may be even higher than the already alarming statistics due to the diagnostic issues we have already discussed. The fact that anxiety is a part of many autistic people's daily lives, however, can sometimes be used to diminish and trivialize its very real impact. This may be amplified further by gender stereotypes that portray anxiety as a 'female' trait which, in turn, could mean that an autistic girl or woman's anxiety is not detected or is seen as unremarkable and not worthy of further investigation or support, unless she reaches a crisis point.

One of the biggest misconceptions around the overlap between anxiety and autism is that since the anxiety often stems from the autistic person's difficulty with living in environments that are not sensitive to their needs, it doesn't require support or treatment, but a readjustment on the autistic person's part, where they should supposedly learn to tolerate the stressors of a neurotypical world. This is a potentially very harmful assumption to make – the impact of long-term, chronic, daily heightened state of alert should not be underestimated and just accepted as something the child should 'get on with' simply because it is common. While saying that being anxious is 'not unusual' in autistic people is factually true and may be a well-intentioned way of normalizing mental health difficulties, it can also be used to dismiss and shut down any further discussions about how the autistic person needs to be supported. Specifically, we need to be cautious of accounts of anxiety in autistic people that firmly position the anxiety as an individual, 'within-person' difficulty, rather than as something that is heavily influenced, or sometimes even caused, by the environment and the experience of living in a neurotypical world. Instead of saying 'This is normal, we all feel anxious at times', it would be more open and validating to acknowledge the young person's difficulty – 'I'm so sorry to hear that – that must be very difficult for you and I really appreciate your telling me. Shall we have a think together about what I can do to make things easier for you?'

Anxiety can take many different forms and it may not always be immediately obvious, particularly in autistic people who mask their differences. In others, the anxiety may manifest itself in a seemingly distinct condition, such as selective mutism (also sometimes referred to as 'situational mutism') – an anxiety-based response where a person is unable to speak in certain contexts, e.g., in the classroom, but is able to communicate fluently in other 'safe' contexts, e.g., at home or in the company of friends.

It is also important to acknowledge that autistic people's

anxiety can reflect very real fears based on experience, such as anticipating the need to engage in 'small talk' during lunch or break time and navigate complex social dynamics or the noise and crowds of being in a shopping centre. In this context, autistic people's anxieties shouldn't be treated as an irrational fear that is not grounded in reality; rather, we need to *proactively* try to identify possible triggers with the young person in order to reduce their impact.

## School distress, school anxiety or emotionally-based school non-attendance

Most children and young people spend, or are expected to spend, a significant proportion of their lives during term-time in school. For some of them, however, going to school and being in school can be so severely distressing, and even traumatizing, that they are struggling to attend. Over the years, this difficulty has been called a variety of names, with the most common ones being 'school refusal', 'school avoidance', 'school reluctance' or 'non-attendance'. Some of these terms, however, are far from neutral – 'refusal', for example, implies an active choice – and possibly even an element of defiance, which could suggest that the child's difficulties are a personal choice that they are in control of, rather than something that they cannot do due to the level of distress they are in.

Researchers Sophie Connolly and Sinéad Mullally have recently come up with the term 'school distress' (SD) as an alternative – and arguably more neutral and factual – way of describing 'a young person's difficulty attending school due to the emotional distress experienced as a result of school attendance'.[59] They also found that autistic people were a staggering 47 times more likely to experience school distress compared to non-autistic pupils.[60] Indeed, a study by Sophie Connolly and colleagues found that an alarming 83.4 per cent of children and young people experiencing school distress were autistic.[61] Connolly and Mullally also identified a concerning trend where the parents of children who experience school distress felt blamed and disbelieved by professionals:

> Parents of children experiencing SD reported overwhelmingly negative treatment from professionals, whereby they frequently reported feeling blamed for their child's difficulties, threatened with fines or court action, spoken to in a dismissive and critical manner, and feeling threatened, vulnerable, and disbelieved following interactions with school staff and other professionals (including Children's Social Services, Local Authorities, and CAMHS staff).[62]

These findings are unlikely to come as a surprise to autistic people, their families and professionals in the field. In my experience, school distress is one of the most persistently misunderstood difficulties autistic children and young people experience. Often, the link between the young person's underlying anxiety and the potentially disastrous consequences of attempts to enforce school attendance is rarely acknowledged fully. The belief that the young person is 'choosing' not to attend school can also lead to misguided and potentially very harmful interventions, such as insistence that they are brought to school against their will, in the hope that they will settle and get acclimatized to being on the school premises.

Intentionally or not, this approach isn't too dissimilar to exposure therapy, where a person with a phobia is presented with an object or situation they find challenging in order to become desensitized to it until it no longer evokes the same response. While this approach can work with irrational or unfounded (but nevertheless very distressing) fears or phobias, such as a fear of spiders, for example, applying it in the context of a highly distressed young person who has likely reached a breaking point is not appropriate. Additionally, we need to acknowledge that, in this context, autistic young people's fears and anxieties may well be perfectly rational and justified. For example, if an autistic girl is overwhelmed by the noise, smells and other sensory challenges she encounters at school, as well as by the upcoming exams and friendship difficulties, these are not irrational fears. Those experiences are objectively distressing for her and we need to look for ways of addressing them, rather than arguing that 'she can do it' because she is 'resilient', for example. We also need to consider how '100% attendance awards' can further contribute to anxiety in autistic children. Having a blanket attendance policy with no room for discretion as far as individual needs are concerned in terms of both the rewards (attendance awards) and punishment (parental prosecution through the courts) can be actively harmful to some autistic children and young people, who are unable, rather than unwilling, to attend school. A bespoke, differentiated and individualized approach is required in those instances. As far as autism and school attendance is concerned, one size truly doesn't fit all – in fact, one size fits no one.

While there is no specific research looking at the most commonly used terminology, in my experience, the terms 'school refusal' and 'school refuser' are still used regularly and casually in conversations. This is problematic, and the issues with these terms are about more than just semantics or being 'overly sensitive' about language – they are, quite simply, misleading. To use an imperfect analogy, calling a child who is not attending school because of debilitating anxiety a 'school refuser' is not too dissimilar to calling a person with an injured leg a 'marathon refuser' – it is inaccurate and wrongly emphasizes a perceived choice that is simply not there at that moment in time.

In light of what we already know about autistic burnout and the elevated risk of mental health difficulties, self-harm and suicide in autistic young women, the importance of taking a carefully planned, well thought-out and empathetic approach to school distress cannot be overstated. Regardless of our underlying intentions or belief that education is important – which it undoubtedly is – we must always take a flexible, 'whole-person' approach. Education is, indeed, important, but so is safeguarding autistic children and young people by ensuring that they are not put in situations that result in such distress that they become burnt out, depressed and have thoughts of harming themselves. No child will be able to engage with learning to the best of their ability if they are in distress, even if they are physically present on the school premises – the best way of making sure that an autistic young person can attend school is to create an environment where they feel safe, understood, listened to and where their needs are recognized and met consistently.

## Eating disorders and autistic girls

Various studies have found a striking overlap – while autism is diagnosed in less than 1 per cent of women in the general population,[63] between 20 and 35 per cent of young women with anorexia meet the diagnostic threshold for autism or have autistic traits[64] – a correlation which is unlikely to occur by chance. However, establishing the causal root is not a straightforward process – does the body's response to starvation and malnourishment result in symptoms that closely resemble autistic traits, as some have suggested, or does autism, with its associated sensory needs and difficulties around cognitive flexibility, facilitate the development of restrictive eating patterns?

These challenges to diagnosis of autism in girls may therefore mean that some girls and women's possible autistic traits may not have been detected until they came to the attention of eating disorder services. To complicate matters further, eating disorders themselves are often underreported and underdiagnosed, potentially creating a double barrier to the detection of these difficulties in girls and women and to establishing the prevalence of autism in individuals with eating disorders. We also need to question our own assumptions about what eating disorders are, and how they may differ in autistic people. For example, a relatively new diagnosis that is believed to affect more autistic people is Avoidant Restrictive Food Intake Disorder (ARFID). While eating disorders are traditionally associated with concerns about body weight and shape, people diagnosed with ARFID may eat an extremely limited diet in terms of the amount and type of food they consume, without any specific concerns about body weight or image. Rather, in the case of ARFID, the restricted or very selective eating patterns may be triggered by other factors unrelated to body image, such as sensory processing differences – for example, increased sensitivity to the texture, smell, colour or temperature of food, or to the feeling of a full stomach.

The links between autism in women and eating disorders are complex and cannot be traced to a single causal factor. Autistic women have reported a range of difficulties with eating[65] – some of these have to do with the sensory properties of food, others have to do with rigid and stereotypical behaviour (such as having specific rituals around eating) or social difficulties (for example, adapting their behaviour while eating around others). However, determining *which* of these factors are the leading causes of eating disorders has proven challenging. At face value, sensory needs seem like a strong candidate, as they could explain both the restrictive eating patterns associated with anorexia and the need to purge, associated with bulimia, due to an unpleasant feeling of stomach fullness.

However, some studies have shown that the presence of sensory processing difficulties is a less reliable predictor of eating disorders than restrictive and repetitive behaviours.[66] This is, at first look, surprising because autistic women tend to show fewer repetitive behaviours than autistic men, which could be hard to reconcile with the increased prevalence of eating disorders in autistic women. An alternative explanation could be that restrictive eating is *precisely* one of the ways repetitive behaviours manifest in women – and that they are not recognized as such by practitioners who are looking for more stereotypically 'male' behaviours.

Finally, Schröder *et al.* have also proposed that emotional regulation could play a role in the overlap between autism and eating disorders.[67] As we have seen, autistic women are more likely to experience sensory and emotional overwhelm and to struggle with recognizing and regulating their emotions, which is where behaviours involving the consumption or restriction of food could provide a coping mechanism. Some autistic people could be relying on emotional eating as a source of positive stimulation (leading to the pattern of bingeing and purging characteristic of bulimia), while others could try to cope with sensory overwhelm in other areas of daily life by withholding food altogether (in a pattern similar to anorexia).

Apart from the causes of the higher rates of eating disorders among autistic women, we should also be mindful that they might face additional challenges in accessing support compared to their neurotypical peers. One survey comparing the experiences of 110 neurotypical and 46 autistic women with eating disorders illustrates some of these difficulties.[68] The autistic women in the study reported experiencing symptoms around age 15 and receiving a diagnosis at age 18, on average – significantly earlier than non-autistic women (17 years old at symptom onset, 22 at diagnosis), and they also experienced these difficulties for longer. More importantly, they rated their experience of specialist support as less beneficial than neurotypical women. Part of this, such as the lower efficacy of dietetic input, could be due to lack of specialist knowledge among practitioners of autistic women's needs. Other interventions, such as Cognitive Behavioural Therapy (CBT), have been developed with the needs of neurotypical clients in mind – such as tackling their presumed concern with weight and body shape – and would require adaptation to fit the profile and particular eating difficulties of autistic women.

## Misdiagnosis and diagnostic overshadowing

I experienced three years of being under the care of Child and Adolescent Mental Health Services exploring issues I had around anxiety, depression and trauma before someone realized there was something else going on. I was then put on the waiting list for an autism assessment and ended up being 'fast tracked' as I was ageing out of services. It all happened in a blur until I did the assessment and was sent off home to await the outcome six weeks later. The report wasn't the most sensitively written thing I've ever had, which was a shame given how much time you spend with ADOS assessors only to have them detail everything you do wrong or differently and not the strengths you have.

*SO, autistic woman*

---

'Diagnostic overshadowing' is defined as 'the misattribution of symptoms of one illness to an already diagnosed comorbidity'.[69] In simple terms, this means that when a person is given a diagnosis, all their difficulties or symptoms could be interpreted as a sign of this *primary diagnosis*, and no alternatives – or additional explanations or diagnoses – are considered.

As we discovered in Chapter 1, autistic girls' needs are often identified significantly later in life compared to boys even when they have a similar presentation, such as high anxiety levels and a tendency to internalize their difficulties. This leads to diagnostic delay and autistic girls may have accumulated multiple other diagnoses prior to being assessed for autism. Those could reflect just one aspect of their difficulties that is particularly pronounced in that moment in time (e.g., anxiety, an eating disorder), or may be wrong altogether (interpreting the overwhelm and distress that is experienced due to sensory overload, difficulties around making sense of other people and one's own emotions and intensive emotional reactions as symptoms of 'emerging personality disorder', for example).

That is not to say that the other diagnosis is not legitimate *per se* – as we have already established, autism can and does co-occur with a range of other conditions and they are not mutually exclusive. For example, a diagnosis of anxiety is likely to reflect the very real anxiety and distress experienced by many autistic people; however, the anxiety may also be directly linked to the autistic person not having their needs met due to the undiagnosed autism. Similarly, years of daily masking may have led to autistic burnout, which could be interpreted as depression, with no regard for the environmental factors, including sensory overload, which have led to it. The primary diagnosis, while not necessarily inaccurate, could then inadvertently become an additional barrier to obtaining an autism diagnosis – it may seem as though there is already 'an answer' that explains their difficulties, and no alternatives are considered.

However, if the autism remains unrecognized, the child or young person could be offered support that is not suitable for neurodivergent people, or for their own specific set of strengths and needs. For example, referring an autistic young woman with social communication difficulties who camouflages those and her anxiety to a group intervention for anxiety may lead to an increase in her masking and anxiety levels, unless suitable adaptations are made and her views are sought. The UK's National Institute for Health and Care Excellence (NICE) has recognized this and has guidelines that clearly state the need for an adapted approach to psychological treatments for autistic people:

> The clinical features and cognitive differences characteristic of ASD mean autistic people require adaptations to standard evidence-based psychological treatments to adequately meet their needs (NICE, 2012). Such adaptations include an increased use of written and visual information, emphasising behaviour change over cognitive approaches, having well explained guidance and rules in therapy, involving a friend, family member or carer, having breaks, incorporating special interests and avoiding ambiguous use of language (Anderson and Morris, 2006; NICE, 2012).[70]

The impact of delayed, wrong or no diagnosis on autistic girls' mental health cannot be underestimated. A 2021 study carried out by researcher Gray Atherton and colleagues looked at the link between age of diagnosis and quality of life; they found that:

> those who received diagnoses later in life were experiencing more mental health challenges... [D]espite academic and professional success, participants were painfully aware of how they struggled socially without knowing why, and this led in many instances to depression, anxiety and even victimization.[71]

This is a particularly important consideration for autistic girls and women, who are more likely to get diagnosed in adulthood – indeed, the same team of researchers found that nearly 60 per cent of autistic women were diagnosed in adulthood, compared to just under 35 per cent of men.[72] The ratios are almost perfectly reversed – the vast majority (or around two thirds) of autistic women get diagnosed in adulthood, whereas the vast majority (again, around two thirds) of autistic men get diagnosed in childhood.

# Conclusion

We cannot fully understand autistic girls' and, indeed, autistic people's needs, unless we take a 'whole person' approach to both recognizing their strengths, difficulties and differences, and supporting them. This task can be complicated immensely by a combination of a lack of awareness, overstretched services that don't always 'talk to each other' and perhaps even a tendency to look for simple answers to complicated questions and supposedly cost-effective 'one size fits all' interventions. We all need to do better than that. We need to be much more proactive, rather than reactive, in identifying when we don't know or understand enough about what a child or a young person's needs are, and in positioning autistic people's voices at the centre of any plan, strategy or intervention.

While some progress has been made in the past 10 years towards a better understanding of the needs of autistic people who mask their differences and difficulties – a presentation particularly common in autistic girls and women – we still have a very long way to go. Now is not the time to be complacent because 'things are changing' – in many respects, they very much haven't changed. Autistic pupils are nearly 47 times more likely to experience school distress, compared to non-autistic young people. Autistic women are 13 times more likely to die by suicide than non-autistic women. The picture is just as alarming when we look at the statistics for autistic people in general, regardless of gender – autistic people are at a significantly higher risk of depression, anxiety, self-harm and suicide than their non-autistic peers.

And yet, the onus can fall overwhelmingly on autistic young people and their families to fight for their own rights, in systems that have not been designed with their needs in mind and that can be surprisingly resistant to change. This is an exhausting and often demoralizing process, especially when combined with the challenges some autistic people have to navigate on a daily basis.

But it is not all doom and gloom – it is true that, in recent years, research, books and discussions about masked or camouflaged autism have become more common, often down to the hard work of actually autistic people who are spreading awareness of this often hidden presentation. This valuable knowledge, and the necessary actions, will need to become embedded in the very systems that are usually present in autistic children's lives – health, social care, local authority and education. However, the bigger and more inflexible a system is, the less likely it is to change easily, quickly or on its own – some may require considerable additional funding, others a major cultural change, or a combination of the two.

In an ideal world, this would be a priority for any government to address, regardless of which side of the political spectrum they are on. Unfortunately, we don't live in an ideal world – and while those changes are taking place, often frustratingly slowly, someone needs to make sure that no autistic child flies under the radar or slips through the proverbial net (and some of those nets have very big gaps indeed). Those of us who are family members, parents or friends of autistic young people – or, indeed, autistic young people themselves – will be well-versed in the challenges this poses, and the amount of time and energy required to advocate on your or your loved one's behalf. But this is also down to those of us who work within those very systems – whether we are teachers, psychologists, therapists, medical professionals, social workers or local authority officers, we hold this responsibility collectively. All of us need to advocate tirelessly for autistic children and young people's needs to be recognized and supported in a timely and efficient manner – because the stakes are just too high.

Finally, to all the incredible autistic young people I have worked with over the years – you have taught me more than any degree or qualification. I hope that we soon live in a world where the ideas presented in this book have become such common knowledge that there is no longer a need for it.

# Endnotes

1   Milton, D. (2012). On the ontological status of autism: The 'Double Empathy Problem'. *Disability and Society, 27*(6), 883–887.
2   Milton, D. (2018). The double empathy problem. *National Autistic Society.* www.autism.org.uk/advice-and-guidance/professional-practice/double-empathy
3   Sheppard, E., Pillai, D., Wong, G.T-L., Ropar, D. & Mitchell, P. (2016). How easy is it to read the minds of people with autism spectrum disorder? *Journal of Autism and Developmental Disorders, 46,* 1247–1254. Cited in Milton, D. (2018). The double empathy problem. *National Autistic Society.* www.autism.org.uk/advice-and-guidance/professional-practice/double-empathy
4   McCrossin, R. (2022). Finding the true number of females with autistic spectrum disorder by estimating the biases in initial recognition and clinical diagnosis. *Children, 9*(2), 272–290.
5   Hirvikoski, T., Boman, M., Chen, Q., D'Onofrio, B.M. *et al.* (2020). Individual risk and familial liability for suicide attempt and suicide in autism: A population-based study. *Psychological Medicine, 50*(9), 1463–1474.
6   Lai, M.C., Lombardo, M.V., Ruigrok, A.N., Chakrabarti, B. *et al.* (2017). Quantifying and exploring camouflaging in men and women with autism. *Autism, 21*(6), 690–702.
7   Mandy, W., Pellicano, L., St Pourcain, B., Skuse, D. & Heron, J. (2018). The development of autistic social traits across childhood and adolescence in males and females. *Journal of Child Psychology and Psychiatry, 59*(11), 1143–1151.

8   Sedgewick, F., Hill, V., Yates, R., Pickering, L. & Pellicano, E. (2016). Gender differences in the social motivation and friendship experiences of autistic and non-autistic adolescents. *Journal of Autism and Developmental Disorders, 46,* 1297–1306.

9   Munroe, A. & Dunleavy, M. (2023). Recognising autism in girls within the education context: reflecting on the internal presentation and the diagnostic criteria. *Irish Educational Studies, 42*(4), 561–581.

10  Duvekot, J., van der Ende, J., Verhulst, F. C., Slappendel, G. *et al.* (2017). Factors influencing the probability of a diagnosis of autism spectrum disorder in girls versus boys. *Autism, 21*(6), 646–658.

11  Mandy, W., Chilvers, R., Chowdhury, U., Salter, G. *et al.* (2012). Sex differences in autism spectrum disorder: evidence from a large sample of children and adolescents. *Journal of autism and developmental disorders, 42,* 1304–1313.

12  Dworzynski, K., Ronald, A., Bolton, P. & Happé, F. (2012). How different are girls and boys above and below the diagnostic threshold for autism spectrum disorders? *Journal of the American Academy of Child & Adolescent Psychiatry, 51*(8), 788–797.

13  Cook, J., Hull, L., Crane, L. & Mandy, W. (2021). Camouflaging in autism: A systematic review. *Clinical Psychology Review, 89,* 102080. Cooper, K., Loades, M.E. & Russell, A. (2018). Adapting psychological therapies for autism. *Research in Autism Spectrum Disorders, 45,* 43–50.

14  Whitlock, A., Fulton, K., Lai, M.C., Pellicano, E. & Mandy, W. (2020). Recognition of girls on the autism spectrum by primary school educators: An experimental study. *Autism Research, 13*(8), 1358–1372.

15  American Psychiatric Association (2013). *Diagnostic and Statistical Manual of Mental Disorders,* 5th edition (DSM-5). Washington, DC: APA.

16  McFayden, T.C., Antezana, L., Albright, J., Muskett, A. & Scarpa, A. (2020). Sex differences in an autism spectrum disorder diagnosis: Are restricted repetitive behaviors and interests the key? *Review Journal of Autism and Developmental Disorders, 7,* 119–126.

17  Supekar, K. & Menon, V. (2015). Sex differences in structural organization of motor systems and their dissociable links with repetitive/restricted behaviors in children with autism. *Molecular Autism, 6*(1), 1–13.

18  Stroth, S., Tauscher, J., Wolff, N., Küpper, C. *et al.* (2022). Phenotypic differences between female and male individuals with suspicion of autism spectrum disorder. *Molecular Autism, 13*(1), 11.

19  O'Nions, E., Petersen, I., Buckman, J.E., Charlton, R. *et al.* (2023). Autism in England: Assessing underdiagnosis in a population-based

cohort study of prospectively collected primary care data. *The Lancet Regional Health – Europe, 29.*

20  Stephens, M. (2023). Fears teenagers self-diagnose autism and ADHD using Tik-Tok. *The Telegraph*, 10 February. www.telegraph.co.uk/news/2023/02/10/fears-teenagers-self-diagnose-autism-adhd-using-tiktok

21  Plummer, K. (2023). Inside TikTok's damaging self-diagnosis trend. *The Independent*, 13 May. www.indy100.com/tiktok/tiktok-self-diagnosis-mental-health

22  Demetriou, E.A., DeMayo, M.M. & Guastella, A.J. (2019). Executive function in autism spectrum disorder: History, theoretical models, empirical findings, and potential as an endophenotype. *Frontiers in Psychiatry, 10,* 753.

23  Johnston, K., Murray, K., Spain, D., Walker, I. & Russell, A. (2019). Executive function: Cognition and behaviour in adults with autism spectrum disorders (ASD). *Journal of Autism and Developmental Disorders, 49,* 4181–4192.

24  Wood-Downie, H., Wong, B., Kovshoff, H., Cortese, S. & Hadwin, J.A. (2021). Research Review: A systematic review and meta-analysis of sex/gender differences in social interaction and communication in autistic and nonautistic children and adolescents. *Journal of Child Psychology and Psychiatry, 62*(8), 922–936.

25  Smith, B.W., Tooley, E.M., Christopher, P.J. & Kay, V.S. (2010). Resilience as the ability to bounce back from stress: A neglected personal resource? *The Journal of Positive Psychology, 5*(3), 166–176.

26  Allen, M. (2014). *Building children and young people's resilience in schools.* Health Equity Briefing 2: September. Public Health England.

27  Sedgewick, F., Hill, V., Yates, R., Pickering, L. & Pellicano, E. (2016). Gender differences in the social motivation and friendship experiences of autistic and non-autistic adolescents. *Journal of Autism and Developmental Disorders, 46,* 1297–1306.

28  Sedgewick, F., Hill, V. & Pellicano, E. (2019). 'It's different for girls': Gender differences in the friendships and conflict of autistic and neurotypical adolescents. *Autism, 23*(5), 1119–1132.

29  Sedgewick, F., Hill, V., Yates, R., Pickering, L. & Pellicano, E. (2016). Gender differences in the social motivation and friendship experiences of autistic and non-autistic adolescents. *Journal of Autism and Developmental Disorders, 46,* 1297–1306.

30  Kuo, M.H., Orsmond, G.I., Cohn, E.S. & Coster, W.J. (2013). Friendship characteristics and activity patterns of adolescents with an autism spectrum disorder. *Autism, 17*(4), 481–500.

31  Dean, M., Harwood, R. & Kasari, C. (2017). The art of camouflage: Gender differences in the social behaviors of girls and boys with autism-spectrum disorder. *Autism, 21*(6), 678–689.

32  Sedgewick, F., Crane, L., Hill, V. & Pellicano, E. (2019). Friends and lovers: The relationships of autistic and neurotypical women. *Autism in Adulthood, 1*(2), 112–123.

33  Sedgewick, F., Crane, L., Hill, V. & Pellicano, E. (2019). Friends and lovers: The relationships of autistic and neurotypical women. *Autism in Adulthood, 1*(2), 112–123.

34  Sedgewick, F., Hill, V. & Pellicano, E. (2019). 'It's different for girls': Gender differences in the friendships and conflict of autistic and neurotypical adolescents. *Autism, 23*(5), 1119–1132.

35  Hadjikhani, N. (2014). Scientifically deconstructing some of the myths regarding autism. *Schweizer Archiv fur Neurologie und Psychiatrie, 165*(8), 272–276.

36  Hadjikhani, N. (2014). Scientifically deconstructing some of the myths regarding autism. *Schweizer Archiv fur Neurologie und Psychiatrie, 165*(8), 272–276.

37  Starita, F. & Di Pellegrino, G. (2018). Alexithymia and the reduced ability to represent the value of aversively motivated actions. *Frontiers in Psychology, 9*, 2587.

38  Hadjikhani, N. (2014). Scientifically deconstructing some of the myths regarding autism. *Schweizer Archiv fur Neurologie und Psychiatrie, 165*(8), 272–276.

39  Hadjikhani, N. (2014). Scientifically deconstructing some of the myths regarding autism. *Schweizer Archiv fur Neurologie und Psychiatrie, 165*(8), 272–276.

40  Sedgewick, F., Crane, L., Hill, V. & Pellicano, E. (2019). Friends and lovers: The relationships of autistic and neurotypical women. *Autism in Adulthood, 1*(2), 112–123.

41  Sedgewick, F., Crane, L., Hill, V. & Pellicano, E. (2019). Friends and lovers: The relationships of autistic and neurotypical women. *Autism in Adulthood, 1*(2), 112–123.

42  Kock, E., Strydom, A., O'Brady, D. & Tantam, D. (2019). Autistic women's experience of intimate relationships: The impact of an adult diagnosis. *Advances in Autism, 5*(1), 38–49.

43  Steward, R., Crane, L., Roy, E.M., Remington, A. & Pellicano, E. (2020). 'Life is much more difficult to manage during periods': Autistic experiences of menstruation. *The Palgrave Handbook of Critical Menstruation Studies*, 751–761.

44  Hirvikoski, T., Boman, M., Chen, Q., D'Onofrio, B.M. *et al.* (2020). Individual risk and familial liability for suicide attempt and suicide in autism: A population-based study. *Psychological Medicine, 50*(9), 1463–1474.

45  Martini, M.I., Kuja-Halkola, R., Butwicka, A., Du Rietz, E. *et al.* (2022). Sex differences in mental health problems and psychiatric hospitalization in autistic young adults. *JAMA Psychiatry, 79*(12), 1188–1198.

46  Anderson, P. (2023). Autism tied to higher rates of self-harm, suicide. *Medscape*, 8 August. www.medscape.com/viewarticle/995275

47  Connolly, S.E., Constable, H. & Mullally, S.L. (2023). School distress and the school attendance crisis: A story dominated by neurodivergence and unmet need. *Frontiers in Psychiatry, 14*, 1237052.

48  Starita, F. & Di Pellegrino, G. (2018). Alexithymia and the reduced ability to represent the value of aversively motivated actions. *Frontiers in Psychology, 9*, 2587.

49  Kinnaird, E., Stewart, C. & Tchanturia, K. (2019). Investigating alexithymia in autism: A systematic review and meta-analysis. *European Psychiatry, 55*, 80–89.

50  Raymaker, D.M., Teo, A.R., Steckler, N.A., Lentz, B. *et al.* (2020). 'Having all of your internal resources exhausted beyond measure and being left with no clean-up crew': Defining autistic burnout. *Autism in Adulthood, 2*(2), 132–143.

51  Raymaker, D.M., Teo, A.R., Steckler, N.A., Lentz, B. *et al.* (2020). 'Having all of your internal resources exhausted beyond measure and being left with no clean-up crew': Defining autistic burnout. *Autism in Adulthood, 2*(2), 132–143.

52  Higgins, J.M., Arnold, S.R., Weise, J., Pellicano, E. & Trollor, J.N. (2021). Defining autistic burnout through experts by lived experience: Grounded Delphi method investigating #AutisticBurnout. *Autism, 25*(8), 2356–2369.

53  Arnold, S.R., Higgins, J.M., Weise, J., Desai, A., Pellicano, E. & Trollor, J.N. (2023). Confirming the nature of autistic burnout. *Autism*. [advance online publication]

54  Mantzalas, J., Richdale, A.L. & Dissanayake, C. (2022). A conceptual model of risk and protective factors for autistic burnout. *Autism Research, 15*(6), 976–987.

55  Martini, M.I., Kuja-Halkola, R., Butwicka, A., Du Rietz, E. *et al.* (2022). Sex differences in mental health problems and psychiatric hospitalization in autistic young adults. *JAMA Psychiatry, 79*(12), 1188–1198.

56  Uljarević, M., Hedley, D., Rose-Foley, K., Magiati, I. *et al.* (2020). Anxiety and depression from adolescence to old age in autism spectrum disorder. *Journal of Autism and Developmental Disorders, 50,* 3155–3165.

57  Higgins, J.M., Arnold, S.R., Weise, J., Pellicano, E. & Trollor, J.N. (2021). Defining autistic burnout through experts by lived experience: Grounded Delphi method investigating #AutisticBurnout. *Autism, 25*(8), 2356–2369

58  Lai, M.C., Saunders, N.R., Huang, A., Artani, A. *et al.* (2023). Self-harm events and suicide deaths among autistic individuals in Ontario, Canada. *JAMA Network Open, 6*(8), e2327415.

59  Connolly, S. & Mullally, S.L. (2023). School distress in UK school children: The parental lived experience. [pre-print] *medRxiv:* www.medrxiv.org/content/10.1101/2023.02.16.23286034v1

60  Connolly, S. & Mullally, S.L. (2023). School distress in UK school children: The parental lived experience. [pre-print] *medRxiv:* www.medrxiv.org/content/10.1101/2023.02.16.23286034v1

61  Connolly, S.E., Constable, H. & Mullally, S.L. (2023). School distress and the school attendance crisis: A story dominated by neurodivergence and unmet need. *Frontiers in Psychiatry, 14,* 1237052.

62  Connolly, S. & Mullally, S.L. (2023). School distress in UK school children: The parental lived experience. [pre-print] *medRxiv:* www.medrxiv.org/content/10.1101/2023.02.16.23286034v1

63  Loomes, R., Hull, L. & Mandy, W.P.L. (2017). What is the male-to-female ratio in Autism Spectrum Disorder? A systematic review and meta-analysis. *Journal of the American Academy of Child and Adolescent Psychiatry, 56*(6), 466–474.

64  Westwood, H. & Tchanturia, K. (2017). Autism spectrum disorder in anorexia nervosa: An updated literature review. *Current Psychiatry Reports, 19*(7), 41.

65  Schröder, S.S., Danner, U.N., Spek, A.A. & van Elburg, A.A. (2022). Problematic eating behaviours of autistic women – A scoping review. *European Eating Disorders Review, 30*(5), 510–537.

66  Bitsika, V. & Sharpley, C.F. (2018). Specific aspects of repetitive and restricted behaviours are of greater significance than sensory processing difficulties in eating disturbances in high-functioning young girls with ASD. *Journal of Developmental and Physical Disabilities, 30*(2), 259–267. Cited in Schröder, S.S., Danner, U.N., Spek, A.A. & van Elburg, A.A. (2022). Problematic eating behaviours of autistic women – A scoping review. *European Eating Disorders Review, 30*(5), 510–537.

67 Schröder, S.S., Danner, U.N., Spek, A.A. & van Elburg, A.A. (2022). Problematic eating behaviours of autistic women – A scoping review. *European Eating Disorders Review, 30*(5), 510–537.

68 Babb, C., Brede, J., Jones, C.R., Serpell, L., Mandy, W. & Fox, J. (2022). A comparison of the eating disorder service experiences of autistic and non-autistic women in the UK. *European Eating Disorders Review, 30*(5), 616–627.

69 Hallyburton, A. (2022). Diagnostic overshadowing: An evolutionary concept analysis on the misattribution of physical symptoms to pre-existing psychological illnesses. *International Journal of Mental Health Nursing, 31*(6), 1360–1372.

70 Cooper, K., Loades, M.E. & Russell, A. (2018). Adapting psychological therapies for autism. *Research in Autism Spectrum Disorders, 45*, 43–50.

71 Atherton, G., Edisbury, E., Piovesan, A. & Cross, L. (2021). Autism through the ages: A mixed methods approach to understanding how age and age of diagnosis affect quality of life. *Journal of Autism and Developmental Disorders, 52*(1), 1–16.

72 Atherton, G., Edisbury, E., Piovesan, A. & Cross, L. (2021). Autism through the ages: A mixed methods approach to understanding how age and age of diagnosis affect quality of life. *Journal of Autism and Developmental Disorders, 52*(1), 1–16.

# Recommended Reading and Resources

## Autism, girls and diagnosis

Carpenter, B., Happé, F. & Egerton, J. (eds) (2019). *Girls and Autism: Educational, Family and Personal Perspectives.* Routledge.

Castellon, S. (2020). *The Spectrum Girl's Survival Guide: How to Grow Up Awesome and Autistic.* Jessica Kingsley Publishers.

Durà-Vilà, G. (2021). *The Amazing Autistic Brain Cards* by Dr Gloria Durà-Vilà. Jessica Kingsley Publishers. (An activity to help explore autism diagnosis with young people and an excellent tool for finding out more about the young person's world and how they perceive themselves. I have used this very successfully in my practice and this is an activity that can be used by both professionals and family members to facilitate discussions.)

Eaton, J. (2023). *Autism Missed and Misdiagnosed: Identifying, Understanding and Supporting Diverse Autistic Identities.* Jessica Kingsley Publishers.

James, L. (2017). *Odd Girl Out: An Autistic Woman in a Neurotypical World.* Boxtree.

O'Brien, S. (2023). *So, I'm Autistic: An Introduction to Autism for Young Adults and Late Teens.* Jessica Kingsley Publishers.

Wassell, C. (2022). *Nurturing Your Autistic Young Person: A Parent's Handbook to Supporting Newly Diagnosed Teens and Pre-Teens.* Jessica Kingsley Publishers.

## Mental health

Bullivant, F.F. & Woods, S. (2020). *Autism and Eating Disorders in Teens: A Guide for Parents and Professionals.* Jessica Kingsley Publishers.

Eaton, J. (2017). *A Guide to Mental Health Issues in Girls and Young Women on the Autism Spectrum: Diagnosis, Intervention and Family Support.* Jessica Kingsley Publishers.

Tchanturia, K. (ed.) (2021). *Supporting Autistic People with Eating Disorders: A Guide to Adapting Treatment and Supporting Recovery.* Jessica Kingsley Publishers.

## Physical health

Steward, R. (2019). *The Autism-Friendly Guide to Periods.* Jessica Kingsley Publishers.

## School and education

Eaton, J., Gillberg, C., Sturrock, A., O'Hagan, S. *et al.* (2019). *Education and Girls on the Autism Spectrum: Developing an Integrated Approach.* Jessica Kingsley Publishers.

Fricker, E. (2023). *Can't Not Won't: A Story about a Child who Couldn't Go to School.* Jessica Kingsley Publishers.

Rae, T. (2020). *Understanding and Supporting Children and Young People with Emotionally Based School Avoidance (EBSA).* Hinton House Publishers Limited.

Rae, T. & Such, A. (2019). *The ASD Girls' Wellbeing Toolkit: An Evidence-Based Intervention Promoting Mental, Physical & Emotional Health.* Hinton House Publishers Limited.

## 'Unmasking', self-care and living authentically as an autistic person

Belcher, H.L. (2022). *Taking Off the Mask: Practical Exercises to Help Understand and Minimise the Effects of Autistic Camouflaging.* Jessica Kingsley Publishers.

Garvey, N. (2023). *Looking After Your Autistic Self: A Personalised Self-Care Approach to Managing Your Sensory and Emotional Well-Being.* Jessica Kingsley Publishers.

Katy, E. (2024). *Girl Unmasked: How Uncovering My Autism Saved My Life.* Monoray.

Price, D. (2022). *Unmasking Autism: Discovering the New Faces of Neuro-diversity.* Harmony.